A GUIDE TO
BIBLICAL PREACHING

A GUIDE TO BIBLICAL PREACHING

JAMES W. COX

ABINGDON   NASHVILLE

A GUIDE TO BIBLICAL PREACHING

Library of Congress Cataloging in Publication Data

COX, JAMES WILLIAM, 1923–
A guide to biblical preaching.
Includes bibliographical references and index.
1. Preaching. 2. Bible—Homiletical use.
I. Title.
BV4211.2.C64   251   76-13491

ISBN 0-687-16230-0

MANUFACTURED BY THE PARTHENON PRESS AT
NASHVILLE, TENNESSEE, UNITED STATES OF AMERICA

To Patty

PREFACE AND ACKNOWLEDGMENTS

Many persons have contributed to the writing of this book. The place of the Bible in my thoughts and affections, as well as in my preaching and teaching, has a long history. My father read aloud from it daily in our home. My mother, who was a public school teacher, read it privately, and at Christmas she gave each of her pupils, including me, a copy of the New Testament (when that used to be permitted!) inscribed with the words, "May the teachings of this book be your guide through life." Pastors, Sunday school teachers, and many others nourished my growing involvement with the Scriptures.

Professionally, I am indebted to many respected mentors. While these include some I have known only through their books, particularly they are my professors and colleagues in the Southern Baptist Theological Seminary, first of all, and also those in Union Seminary, Princeton Seminary, the University of Zurich, and the Baptist Seminary of Rüschlikon-Zurich, Switzerland.

I am especially grateful to the Trustees and Administration of the Southern Baptist Theological Seminary for providing both encouragement and secretarial help for such projects as this. Miss Alicia Gardner, Supervisor of Office Services, and Mrs. Pat Lee Schmidt, who very painstakingly typed the manuscript, have my hearty thanks.

A special note of acknowledgment is due to Dr. James Cleland, longtime Dean of the Chapel and Professor of

Homiletics at Duke University Divinity School. His sermon adaptations of the concepts of General End and Specific Intent put forth by Alan Monroe in his *Principles and Types of Speech* are reflected in Appendix A, "Examples of Sermon Preliminaries."

James W. Cox

CONTENTS

INTRODUCTION:

HOW TO USE THIS BOOK

This book is for both the practicing preacher and the student preacher. It has the following aims in mind:

- To highlight the values of biblical preaching and the need for it
- To describe and give examples of the wide range of sermons that can be called biblical
- To point the way to the meatiest and most preachable texts of both Testaments
- To show how to unearth the treasures lying in these texts and make them available for sermons
- To help the preacher to find the most effective form in which to structure his message
- To exploit the most effective sources of illustrative material and verbal communication

If these aims appeal to you, I suggest that you do the following:

First, read straight through the book, relating what you read to your current sermons or, if you are not yet a practitioner, to what you think will be helpful to your future ministry.

Second, go over again in depth those parts of the book that are of special interest to you, and begin to make immediate use of any helpful suggestions.

Third, draw up a plan for a program of biblical preaching. Study the lectionary in Appendix C and consider its possibilities for suggestions of texts and themes for one sermon per week. Project a long-range plan. Be presumptuous and set down in broad outline what you would like to do in a pastorate of twenty-five years (or whatever time might be left until retirement); be a bit more detailed and indicate what a five-year program might realistically include; and make a Sunday-by-Sunday schedule of texts and tentative themes for the next year. Make your own lectionary—if that is more serviceable to you—but use the lectionary in this book at least as a checklist to see whether you are habitually neglecting any part of the Bible in your preaching.

Fourth, decide on a systematic way of gathering and preserving materials for your sermons. A notebook listing each text on a separate blank page, or a manila folder for each text will, in the long run, be a valuable time-saver.

Fifth, as the time approaches for the final preparation of the sermon, apply some or all of the questions for the text, as listed in chapter 3. In this connection, it may be helpful to review the "Guiding Principles for the Interpretation of the Bible" in Appendix B. Then, with your material before you, decide on your central idea, general end, and specific intent, as outlined in "Sermon Preliminaries" in Appendix A.

Finally, run through the sample outlines in chapter 4 for suggestions of ways to structure your thoughts so as to best achieve your sermon objective. Review the various forms of textual support (including illustrations) for examples of ways to put flesh on your sermonic skeleton. Try forms you have never used before or have used too little. Then, attempt to put your message in sentences and words that are clear, convincing, warm, and persuasive.

The Epilogue of chapter 5 includes several other suggestions that are particularly relevant to the preacher's continuing, long-range enrichment.

One last, important word: I have tried to show here some very human ways of enhancing our ability to get a hearing for the message of the Bible. Let none of us imagine that psychological and verbal tricks can in any way substitute for the work of God in getting people to understand, to believe, to experience true joy, or to become rightly related to God, others, or self. Yet God has used the common things of earth to reveal his glory, and it is my hope he will increasingly use us who preach his Word as we make ourselves more and more accessible to his purposes through serious examination of our preaching performance and through persistent efforts to improve it.

CHAPTER ONE

WHAT IS BIBLICAL PREACHING?

<u>The Forgotten</u> The Bible is asking to be read, taught, and
<u>Bible</u>   proclaimed. "Stifle yourself," we have said to
it, though perhaps with words more polite. We have read
many books about the Bible or about subjects related to it.
We have spent countless hours with magazines and journals
that deal seriously with the vital spiritual and social issues of
our time. We have joined discussion groups and pooled our
ignorance, prejudices, and occasionally our knowledge and
wisdom, and meanwhile drunk enough coffee to fill a
baptistry. But the Bible itself we have ignored except as a last
resort at sermon-making time.

Why would we do this? We have not stayed with the Bible
long enough to love it in spite of its idiosyncracies, its
elusiveness, its refusal to allow us to sit in judgment on it, its
independence. Like a lover—as Markus Barth has shown
us—the Bible must be wooed before it will reveal its heart to
us.[1] It will not yield to our peremptory demands; it will not
be taken by storm.

So, since for many of us the Bible is like a neighbor we see
and speak to occasionally but don't really know, we act no
more than civilly toward it. The sermon and the biblical text
may live on the same street, but their houses are separate.
Little or no communication goes on between them. And all
the while this neighbor whom it would be so beneficial to

know makes many signs of wishing to get better acquainted, only to be politely but persistently ignored. This ought to change.

I. WHY PREACH FROM THE BIBLE

The Most Inter- The reasons for changing our attitudes to-
esting Material ward the Bible are both practical and theolog-
ical. For one thing, the material in the Bible is by and large the most interesting material you can find. It deals with the deepest conflicts imaginable, ranging all the way from conflict that is cosmic in scope to the domestic quarrel of two brothers over an inheritance. Several years ago, I came across a book that quoted a reference of Goethe to the thirty-six (and only thirty-six) dramatic situations in existence and presumably the only possible ones. Georges Polti had examined the principal dramas of China, India, Judea, and Greece and been able to isolate thirty-six dramatic categories into which all the most interesting stories of the world could be placed.[2] Recently, I went over the list one by one and found in the Bible thirty-five of the thirty-six possible types. Do you know of any single volume or collection so rich in material to capture the attention, stir the imagination, and move the soul?

Fascinating Not only are you faced with a profusion of
Variety different themes and stories in the Bible, but
you are also overwhelmed by the fascinating variety of literary forms. History, poetry, legal statute, proverb, parable, fable, epistle, dialectic, oratory, apocalyptic—they are all there. And they are waiting to be used in their special forms to make your sermons easier to listen to.

With all the variety of content and form of the Bible unfolding before his eyes, no wonder Charles Spurgeon said,

15

"Give me the Bible and the Holy Ghost and I can go on preaching for ever."

The Bible a Part of Us   Consider also that the Bible is a part of our tradition, our heritage, our culture. Can you understand yourself as a Westerner, as an American, as a Christian, or as a Baptist without understanding something of the Bible? Our laws, our morals, our customs, our language, our literature—as well as our religious life—can be in many ways and in many degrees traced to the Bible. The Bible is the seen or unseen guest, the invited or uninvited guest in every home. The Reformation in the sixteenth century brought about popular interest in the Bible. In time, as copies of the Bible became inexpensive enough to be purchased for every home, the Bible became the stronghold of family piety.

A scene not easily found in many homes today is that of a family gathered round to read the Bible, sing, and pray. If there is any gathering at all, it is about the television set. But we may be on the threshold of a better day. Even though the good things do not happen now as we would like to plan them, many good things are taking us by surprise, perhaps startling us so very much by their crude innocence that we are tempted to reject them.

Resurgence of Interest   In recent years we have seen an amazing resurgence of Bible study among groups of young people. Of course, many of them pick out the verses they like and miss a great deal of the rest; they put memorization above understanding; they use the Bible as a glorified crystal ball for gazing presumptuously into secrets known only to God. But isn't that better than not reading the Bible at all? Can't we accept half a loaf? Why not react as Paul did when he heard that some men were preaching Christ out of envy and strife? He thanked God that Christ was being preached, though imperfectly. As a preacher, you have the opportunity to build on the desire for understanding of the written word; you have the opportunity to increase understanding, to correct misunderstanding, and to bring about discovery of the object of the Scriptures—the revelation of the love of God for all mankind in Jesus Christ. So, however accidentally, however mechanically, or however misguidedly people get involved with the Bible, your work is cut out for you—to help these people to a new and fresh involvement with the Bible that is firsthand, heartfelt, and intelligent.

Biblical Authority   Consider further that the Bible gives us authoritative information about our faith. Every church in Christendom claims to find its doctrinal basis in the New Testament—and in the Old. And they are right—all of them. On the main points, we are one; it is the trivial things or the differing emphases on important things that separate us. Other sources may be important for understanding our faith, but the Bible is more important. We test all other sources of faith, inspiration, and information by its fundamental, as well as enduring, standard.

How does the Bible enjoy such authority? It witnesses to the revelation of God through a special history; it is the testimony of those who were closest to what God was revealing; and, by its fruits, it bears the stamp of divine inspiration. A man may find it hard to accept what is to be believed in the Bible, but he should have no trouble in determining—in the main—what was believed by those who wrote it. For that reason, the words of Scripture are to Christians everywhere, of whatever church, holy.

A Catalyst of Encounter   Consider as of utmost importance that the Bible is the catalyst of a divine-human encounter. It makes it possible for a human being to come into transforming contact with God. Paul wrote to Timothy: "From childhood you have been acquainted with the sacred writings which are able to instruct you for salvation through faith in Christ Jesus" (II Tim. 3:15 RSV); and again, "Preach the word, be urgent in season and out of season" (II Tim. 4:2 RSV). It is true, as the Reformation theologian Bullinger averred, "The preaching of the word of God *is* the word of God."[3] Could that be truly said of the preaching of anything else?

Charles R. Brown, longtime dean of Yale Divinity School, reflected once on an encounter with a man who almost by accident attended a Sunday evening service where he was preaching. The man was in the throes of the most acute crisis of his life, and something the preacher said that night made everything new and different. After telling the details, Dr. Brown raised the question, "Suppose that I had been trifling with some fringe of the truth that night!"

In response to some of my own pointed questions, Colonel Ben S. Price, at that time the chief of chaplains at Fort Knox, wrote:

> I definitely think that there is an increasing need and even demand for biblical preaching today as over against topical preaching. I think that our people are about fed up with listening to the personal opinions of individuals from pulpits which fail to be grounded in the eternal truths of God. In my experience, people are far more receptive to a mediocre presentation from the pulpit that is grounded in the Word than they are to a more proficient, more professional job that fails to rest solidly on the Gospel message.[4]

Why is this so? On this I agree profoundly with Alan Richardson, who said, "The Bible is and remains the appointed means of God's conversation with men."[5]

II. HOW TO PREACH FROM THE BIBLE

A Simple If, then, there is a great and persistent need for
Strategy more and better biblical preaching, how can you
do it? Here is a simple strategy.

The Role Begin with a genuine desire to know the Bible. I
of Need intended what I have said so far to be provocative
and to support and strengthen any inclination you may have
toward exploring the advantages of biblical preaching. But
your approach must be like one preaching to the uncon-
verted: you don't ordinarily make a convert the first time you
preach to a man; some crisis arises in the man's life, and
what you have said plus the pressures of need intersect and
lead to change. If you honestly face your personal needs and
sympathetically enter into the needs of those who hear you,
you will, like mice trapped in a maze, go to the only way
out—to the message of the Bible. D. E. King, an outstanding
black preacher, had such an experience. As he looked back,
he said of his Bible reading, "Now I read more between the
lines than I used to read on the lines."[6]

From a Part You will come to an appreciation of the Bible
to the Whole by way of a fresh and vital interest in some part
of it. A verse or an incident strikes fire with you, and then all
things are new. But you may at that point suffer a case of
arrested development. You may make a hobby of one
emphasis, one doctrine, or one part of the Bible and ignore
the rest. All of us have known of preachers who were
handicapped by their preoccupation with evangelism or
worship or election or eschatology or baptism. They
excluded or minimized everything else.

A real love for the word of God, however, will lead you
into a never-ending exploration of the riches tucked away in
every corner of the Bible. It won't suffice for you to take a
mere academic or preferential interest in any one part of it.

Of course, some parts will interest you more than others; you will have your favorite verses, chapters, and books; some parts will address your immediate needs more than others. But you have to see the Bible as a whole in order to savor truly any of its parts. Increasingly I appreciate the suggestion of Professor Knox that in biblical preaching we should stay close to the great themes of the Bible, "the characteristic and essential biblical ideas." [7]

Contribution of Biblical and Systematic Theology When I was still in high school, I was blessed to have a pastor who was interested in me and lent me his books, some of which I am sure he was inclined theologically to rate "X" for my young eyes. My science teacher in high school was a devout churchman and introduced me to the treasures in the county library. So, while still quite young, I read E. Y. Mullins' *Christian Religion in Its Doctrinal Expression* and Harry Emerson Fosdick's *Guide to Understanding the Bible.* The first work confronted me with a contemporary synthesis of the basic biblical ideas; the second, with a statement of the development of leading biblical ideas as they wound their way through the Old Testament and the New. It was a wonderful experience—exciting, disturbing, challenging, and enriching.

Since then I have tried to look at every text from two viewpoints: (1) what it meant in the particular time and circumstances in which it arose and (2) what it means in our present life situation.

Let me suggest now some methods for getting at the content of the Bible so as to make this content available for the production of sermons. Let us assume that you have decided on a biblical text. How can it be induced to come to life? With the help of some of my mentors I have devised a series of questions which I am convinced when applied to a preachable text, lead it to surrender its riches. (These questions are listed and dealt with in detail in chapter 3.)

The Sermon Seminar There is another way. For some it may be the best way of all. Get the help of the people who will hear your sermon. This is in one sense nothing new. Some preachers have discussed their texts with interested individuals. Others have visited and counseled with their parishioners regularly and have noted their needs and problems. In this way they have been able to preach with refreshing relevance. I know of one pastor who often lets one sermon lead to another not by design but on the basis of direct and private feedback from articulate individuals in his congregation. This might go on for weeks while pastor and people struggle together to see the whole truth about an elusive or complex theme. However, the most promising method I have found is the method of the sermon seminar. Get together a group of the people who will hear your sermon. Present the text to them, and then sit back and be quiet and attentive while they discuss the text for an hour and a half. Help them out if they get stuck on some technical point, but encourage them to express the questions the text raises for their own life and times so they might share their insights into the text's practical meaning. If you take their questions and insights seriously, can you fail to preach with excitement? Can you fail to gain and hold an unusual degree of their interest?

H. H. Farmer spoke convincingly when he said:

> Those who have what are called "pulpit gifts" will suffer great loss of power if their preaching is not surrounded by those more direct and intimate personal relations which are part of a faithful pastoral ministry exercised over a number of years. And to succumb to temptation to rely on your pulpit powers to make up for deficiency on the pastoral side is fatal. In the end it leads to what I can only call "French-lacquer" preaching, bright and

interesting, but lacking depth and tenderness and searching power.[8]

<u>The Medium and the Message</u> However, before we get too far with the sermon, we have to raise the question of form. How can the material in the text best be shaped to do its job? You could solve that problem for yourself by forcing every sermon into a rigid, predetermined mold, such as: Faith—Its Nature, Its Sources, and Its Uses. Every sermon would sound just like its predecessor, with each succeeding one duller than the one before. One remedy for that is to let every text have, if possible, its maximum exposure. Get as much of the form of the sermon as you can from the form of the text. The poet John Ciardi was right, I believe, when he gave the title to a collection of his poems *How Does a Poem Mean?* not *What Does a Poem Mean?* For the very "how"—the form, the style—of a poem is often a part of its meaning. So it may be with your sermon. The closer the sermon sticks to the text, the closer it may be to God's intention for its use in a particular situation.

<u>The Oldest Form</u> The most obvious way to do this would seem to be the use of the homily—the verse-by-verse, phrase-by-phrase, or even word-by-word treatment of the text, beginning at the beginning of the text and continuing toward the end in the order in which the separate parts are found in the passage. Augustine, trained as a rhetorician and teacher of rhetoric before becoming a Christian, knew other ways of making a sermon. Occasionally he chose one of those methods. But most of his sermons were homilies, the approach used in the church at the time of his conversion. Others since Augustine have used the same method, and it has much to commend it; it is at one and the same time the easiest to do and the hardest. If you think it easy, you will be superficial, repetitive, and boring; if you come to the

challenge of a passage such as Jacob meeting the angel at Jabbok, you will wrestle with it and not let go until the text blesses both you and those who are under your spiritual care.

However, it would not be wise or helpful to suggest that there are no other methods or—for some preachers—no other more useful and productive methods of preaching biblically. Every preacher ought to get out of his rut occasionally, even though the rut is comfortable and offers a measure of security.

The Power of the Story Why not tell a biblical story or relate a biblical incident, taking care to describe the scenes, delineate the characters, and unfold the drama so that the text comes alive in the sympathies, identifications, and tensions that take hold of the hearer? You can make application by a mere subtle suggestion. There is no need for heavy-handed application on every point or for a moral tacked on at the end. As Markus Barth has observed, "Actually, even in sophisticated suburbs and on egghead campuses a comparably small number of people, if any, would despise the charm of a well told story."[9]

The "Plain Style" Sermon Why not explain or narrate the text in its original setting and then draw its meaning together into one crisp sentence that you can explain, interpret, prove, or illustrate in timeless terms and afterwards apply to the present times or the present congregation? Professor Elton Trueblood has suggested that this is a method by which anybody can prepare a sermon: explain the text; tell what it means; and apply it.[10]

Multiple Texts Again, why not occasionally use multiple texts? The ancient question in the book of Job, "If a man die, shall he live again?" can be answered by Jesus' words in the Fourth Gospel, "He that liveth and believeth in me shall never die." Two of the first questions in both of the

Testaments have been noted to be, "Where *art* thou?" (Gen.
3:9) and "Where is he that is born King of the Jews?" (Matt.
2:2). In a sermon called "Four Judgments on Jesus," W. E.
Sangster brought together these four texts: "Many of them
said, He hath a demon" (John 10:20); "Some said, He is a
good man" (John 7:12); "Simon Peter . . . said, Thou art the
Christ" (Matt. 16:16); "Thomas . . . said . . . , My Lord and
my God" (John 20:28).[11] It does not take much imagination to
recognize these exciting possibilities.

A Paradox of Preaching Let us be clear on this: one does not have to be
bound by the form of the text to preach
biblically! You may, in fact, preach unbiblically with a text
and biblically without one. As you plan to preach a certain
biblical truth or insight, you may take a focal word, phrase,
or verse from a text and reach into the context for whatever is
available to explain and support your focus of discussion.
Or, you may take a text as a particular instance of a general
truth and preach on the general truth. Or, you may go from a
general statement to discuss only one aspect of it. Still
further, you may take a broad theme without a text and trace
it through a Bible book or even throughout the Bible. If a
preacher loves people and the Word of God, he will get them
together one way or another, and the result will be good!

Now here are a few tips on developing the ideas in those
texts.

The Need to Explain 1. Explain what needs explaining, but no more.
Unless it serves your overall objective for the
sermon, don't spend much time explaining geographical,
historical, or archaeological details. And you need not
explain the obvious. Moreover, recognize your human
inability to explain some things. The Bible itself is full of
God, but nowhere does it undertake a systematic explanation
of him or an anxious effort to make men believe in him.

When the apostle Paul takes on the task of justifying the ways of God to man, he breaks off, exclaiming, "O depth of wealth, wisdom, and knowledge in God! How unsearchable his judgments, how untraceable his ways!" (Rom. 11:33 NEB). He tries, and he is to be commended for trying, though he is humble enough and honest enough to recognize his limitations. We should not assume anything. Define your terms; explain your ideas thoroughly. Go as far as your knowledge and the truth of God will permit. James T. Cleland does this well in a sermon on Romans 1:1 entitled "Paul, a Slave of Jesus Christ":

> If there is one name which the average Christian is unwilling to apply to himself—is even squeamish about applying to himself—it is the title "slave." When it comes to a designation like that you and I balk. We may be willing to be called many things for Christ's sake, but "slave of Christ" is hardly one of them. "Slave" is an out-of-date kind of term. What's more, it is a word we would rather forget in the South.
>
> It is interesting that when the King James Version was made in England in the seventeenth century and the Revised Standard Version was made in the United States in the twentieth century, the translators on both occasions, had an aversion to the English word "slave." Doulos, d-o-u-l-o-s, which certainly means a "slave" in Greek, is given a more genteel rendition. Romans 1:1 in the King James Version is: "Paul, a servant of Jesus Christ." That is the Revised Standard Version reading, too, except that "slave" is offered as an alternative in a footnote. But—a slave is a slave. When Paul called himself a doulos of Jesus Christ, he meant that he was Christ's bondsman. Can we be certain of that? Well, listen to his own words in Galatians 6:17, as Moffatt translates them: ". . . I bear branded on my body the owner's stamp of the Lord Jesus." Branded, no less. He speaks again: "You are not your own, you were bought for a price." (1 C. 6:20. cf. 7:23) That describes a transaction in the slave market.
>
> We had better cooperate with the inevitable and accept the face that according to St. Paul, one name for Christian—one name, there are others—is "slave." [12]

25

<u>Achieving</u>   2. Apply the truths you preach; link them up
<u>Relevance</u>   with life as it is lived today; tie them in with the
experience and problems of the people who sit in the pews
before you. That is what Jesus did. So did the apostles and
other New Testament preachers. In that sense, all New
Testament preaching is prophetic, and all worthy preaching
through the centuries has been prophetic. It touches
contemporary life. The editors of the monumental collection
Twenty Centuries of Great Preaching did not choose sermons
according to abstract rhetorical criteria but with regard to a
more significant touchstone:

> Great preaching is relevant preaching. That is not a presupposi-
> tion with which this work was begun, but a conclusion to which
> it came. After studying the lives of hundreds of preachers and
> reading countless sermons, we concluded that the preachers who
> made the greatest impact upon the world were men who spoke to
> the issues and needs of their day.[13]

Look at the sermons by Eduard Schweizer in *God's Inescapable Nearness* or those by Karl Barth in *Deliverance to the
Captives,* and you will see how to let the transforming spirit
of God come to expression through the text from the very
beginning.

In a sermon on Revelation 1:9-20, a text that portrays "one
like a son of man" from whose mouth "issued a sharp
two-edged sword," Schweizer says,

> An early Christian prophet by the name of John tells us how he
> gazed upon the risen Christ and how God himself took hold of his
> life through that experience and met him face to face. But what an
> incredibly strange Jesus it is—this Jesus who is about to meet us
> in the Scripture that records what happened to John! It is a Jesus
> quite different from the one we are accustomed to. But perhaps
> for that very reason he has a bare chance actually to get through to
> us, past all the multitude of things behind which we barricade
> ourselves. Perhaps this time he will be able to approach us in

such a way as to make it impossible for us to say, "Yes, yes, so it is," and then quit listening because we think we already know everything he has to say to us, thanks to the hundreds of hours we have spent listening to sermons, Sunday school lessons, and other kinds of religious instruction. . . .

But this Jesus is not merely the dear Savior in whom we can place our trust. This Jesus is not our brother in such a way that we can clap him on the shoulder and say, "We are pals." This Jesus can be so incredibly strange that we almost die when he actually comes into our life. A Jesus who says, "He who loves father or mother, son or daughter, more than me is not worthy of me," is incredibly strange. A Jesus who leads his disciples into prisons and to the executioner's block, rather than from victory to victory for God's kingdom, is incredibly strange. A Jesus who continues to be the Savior in Auschwitz or in the jungle of Vietnam is incredibly strange. If we can be untroubled and comfortable Christians, then it may be that this Jesus has never yet become a reality in our lives. You and I are not prophets, so we cannot expect him to come to us in the same way he came to John. But what if those many things in our lives that ought to die do not die? What if, instead, they grow and proliferate? If that is the case, we should ask ourselves whether he is actually with us or if perchance up to now we have passed him by.[14]

A Call to
Concreteness
3. Illustrate what you hope the people will learn or do. This is extremely important, for illustrations can serve both to explain and to apply what you are attempting to get across. A well-chosen analogy will enable a hearer to take what he knows and from that leap across to what he does not know or does not know well enough. An example loaded with the realities of the human heart can lead a hearer to want to do what you hold before him as an opportunity or challenge. Besides, the use of pictures of one sort or another is the most interesting way to teach; the use of human interest stories is the most interesting way to impress, convince, and persuade. The preacher who illustrates keeps his congregation awake; the one who deals in unadorned abstractions puts his people to

sleep. This simple truth is so widely neglected that someone has defined a preacher as a man who talks in another person's sleep.

But the matter is more serious than that. It was a noted theologian and preacher who said,

> I believe that abstractness in some ways is the greatest curse of all our preaching. . . . God comes at people not through abstractions at all, but through persons and through the concrete situations of day to day personal life. There is indeed a type of mind, especially of educated mind, which finds great delight in the development and interplay of abstract theological ideas and general theological truths, if it is at all skillfully done, and for such minds it can be a positive snare and danger. The play of ideas screens them from the living God. It is an escape from God the more dangerous because it professes to be an encounter with Him.[15]

The Best Illustrations   Where will you find illustrations? They are everywhere in life about you—things you have observed, heard, and experienced. But the very best ones may come from the Bible itself. When the sermon is largely a story from the Bible, you may need no further illustrative material; the story itself provides the concrete data, the human interest, and the color required for attention, conviction, and impression. Charles Wallis, for many years editor of homiletical materials, comments on the use of Bible illustrations: "As pastors we miss our most important, pertinent, and life-centered resource—the Bible in which the proclamation of the gospel must find its stimulus and inspiration."[16]

The preacher who uses the Bible in his preaching and uses it well has abundant rewards. He can enjoy the assurance that his people are well fed, that they have maximum opportunity to grow in the knowledge of our Lord and Savior

Jesus Christ, and that he as a preacher is fulfilling the apostolic command: "Preach the Word!"

The following chapters are designed to expand, elaborate, and exemplify the most important ideas set forth in this first chapter. Some repetition of these ideas, therefore, is to be expected as they are highlighted in various contexts.

NOTES

1. Markus Barth, *Conversation with the Bible* (New York: Holt, Rinehart and Winston, 1964), pp. 7–10.

2. Georges Polti, *The Thirty-Six Dramatic Situations* (Boston: The Writer, 1940), pp. 7, 10–11.

3. From the Second Helvetic Confession.

4. Price to Cox, January 15, 1973.

5. Alan Richardson, *Preface to Bible Study* (Philadelphia: Westminster Press, 1944), p. 13.

6. Sermon, the Southern Baptist Theological Seminary.

7. John Knox, *The Integrity of Preaching* (New York: Abingdon Press, 1957), p. 19.

8. Herbert H. Farmer, *The Servant of the Word* (Philadelphia: Fortress Press, 1942), p. 67.

9. Markus Barth, "The Cowboy and the Sunday School," *Religious Education,* 57 (January-February, 1962) p. 42.

10. Lecture, Southern Baptist Theological Seminary, February 22, 1963.

11. W. E. Sangster, *Can I Know God?* (New York: Abingdon Press, 1960), p. 62.

12. James T. Cleland, "Paul, a Slave of Jesus Christ," *Sermons of the Week,* 2:44 (March 1, 1961), p. 19.

13. Clyde E. Fant, Jr. and Wm. M. Pinson, eds., *Twenty Centuries of Great Preaching* (Waco: Word Books, 1971), Vol. 1, p. v.

14. Eduard Schweizer, "A Different Kind of Jesus," a sermon trans. by James W. Cox in *Princeton Seminary Bulletin,* 66, No. 1 (October 1973), pp. 55–6.

15. Farmer, *Servant of the Word,* p. 71.

16. Charles L. Wallis, *1010 Sermon Illustrations from the Bible* (New York: Harper & Row, 1963), p. xi.

CHAPTER TWO

USING TEXTS

"I cannot preach without a text." It was not a theological greenhorn speaking, but one of America's most gifted preachers. These words of Harold Cooke Phillips startled his audience of seminary students, for they had heard him preach and recognized his competence in many fields—philosophy, theology, the arts, and current affairs. Yet his Christian heritage and commitment had first claim on him. Therefore, he said, "I cannot preach without a text."

I. THE PURPOSE OF A TEXT

A Logical Starting Point Why have a text? As suggested by the previous chapter, the text provides a logical starting point for the sermon. The Bible is the treasury of the history of our faith. It is our most reliable witness to the objective reality of what we believe. Anything that we might be able to say about our faith is in the Bible—explicitly or by implication. The Bible is the native port from which we sail on the high seas of modern thought and living. We may sail far into the mysteries of modern depth psychology, along the uncertain shores of modern philosophy, into the towering waves of world crises, or upon the more serene ebb and flow of the arts; yet the Bible is our home. A text is the reminder of who we are, where we are going, and what we ought to be doing. Therefore, the text makes every strange sea and shore an extension of our native spiritual home. As Karl Barth noted, "We can no more liberate ourselves from the Bible than a child can liberate himself from his father."[1]

A Generating and Controlling Factor Put another way, the text contains the basic idea and the leading thoughts of the sermon. It will be both a generating factor and a controlling factor as the sermon develops. Many ideas and trains of thought will leap from the text and disport in joyous abandon. However, the text itself will exercise stern discipline over its offspring. It will demand strict obedience to its will. As you plan your sermon, the text will be at once your most creative helper and your most critical judge.

II. TYPES OF TEXTS

The Entire Bible Sermon texts are of many sorts. Believe it or not, the entire Bible may serve as the text of a single sermon. One of the most breathtaking homiletical performances I have ever seen in print is a sermon entitled "The Christ of the Bible," by the Rev. D. J. McDowell, a black preacher.[2] In this sermon he relates Jesus Christ to every book of the Bible individually. Perhaps you would like to give your congregation a sweeping view of the Bible. This may be done from numerous standpoints. You might trace the history of redemption from Genesis to Revelation, though a book-by-book treatment is hardly to be recommended. Or you might show how God takes the initiative in man's redemption. Or you might deal with the Bible's inspiration, its authority, or its purpose. The point is this: you may develop each of these themes in relation to the entire Bible and at the same time give your congregation a key for interpretation.

A Section of the Bible Further, you may narrow the scope of your text. Suppose you choose a section of the Bible. You can show how certain historical books are linked together. You can show and interpret the main concerns of this section. Or, even more interesting, you can focus attention on a central character whose life, words, and deeds figure prominently in the writing: Moses in the Pentateuch, Jesus in the Gospels, Paul in the Acts and the Epistles. Though the scope is narrowed here, it may seem almost impossible to comprehend it in one sermon. But it can be done. And the congregation can make better sense of the details of the material that you have massed together. Excellent examples on sections of the Bible may be found in the old series of volumes entitled *Whyte's Bible Characters,* by Alexander Whyte, and in more recent volumes by Clarence E. Macartney and Clovis Chappell.

A Book   The same principle holds for preaching on an entire book of the Bible. A sermon on a Bible book would attempt to introduce the congregation to the book, to set forth its leading theme or a secondary theme, or to delineate the character of some outstanding person walking through its pages. The little Epistle of Jude or the Third Epistle of John will make an excellent sermon. But so will Genesis or Jeremiah. The following sermon titles by Dwight E. Stevenson suggest interesting thematic treatments:[3]

On Genesis—"Man, Civilization, and God"
On Deuteronomy—"This Nation Under God"
On Ezekiel—"Watchman for the World"
On Hosea—"The Cross of Hosea" (from H. W. Robinson)
On Mark—"Strong Son of God"
On Romans—"Man's Disorder and God's Design"
On I Peter—"Suffering in the Light of the Resurrection"
On Revelation—"Fire on the Earth"

A Section of a Book Also, a sermon on a section of a book would capture the unity of a part of the book within a larger unity.[4] To do this is more fruitful than to handle the book a chapter at a time. Our present use of chapter divisions is to blame for this. Since they do not always break logically, chapter divisions should be ignored and the units of thought should be isolated. Some of the newer translations of the Bible are most helpful here. The New English Bible, for example, sets apart the different sections of a book, and the breaks are quite clear. It divides I Corinthians with these section headings:

> Unity and Order in the Church
> The Christian in a Pagan Society
> Spiritual Gifts
> Life After Death
> Christian Giving

Harry Emerson Fosdick once preached an entire sermon on the Sermon on the Mount, using Matthew 7:14 ("For the gate is narrow and the way is hard, that leads to life, and those who find it are few") as the key verse through which to enter upon the essential teachings of that entire section of Matthew's Gospel.[5]

A Paragraph Andrew W. Blackwood believed that the paragraph is the basic unit of composition in the biblical sermon. It presents just the right amount of material. It will produce a well-rounded message without too much detail. It has perhaps the richest possibilities for consecutive Bible exposition, though even longer units are both acceptable and very usable.[6] *The New Testament in Modern Speech*, translation by Richard Francis Weymouth, gives the paragraph topics in insets and suggests the direction in which the preacher may go as he prepares his sermon. Under the

heading "The Divisions in the Corinthian Church" (I Cor.),
Weymouth lists these paragraph topics:[7]

An Appeal for Unity
The Message of the Cross
Facts as to the Church in Corinth
The True, Divine Wisdom
The Teaching of the Holy Spirit
Divisions a Sure Proof of Unspirituality
Human Teachers Mere Instruments in God's Hands

A Verse   The Bible verse or sentence is the "normal"
or Sentence   Bible unit for sermons. It is sometimes treated
in isolation and thus misinterpreted or misapplied. But if it
becomes the focal point of some larger context, it has
remarkable possibilities. The preacher is never at a loss for
supporting ideas: they are in the context. He never has to be
tedious: he can choose from the context whatever details
serve his aim. The sentence may be an opening through
which the riches of an entire book or at least of the
immediate context may pass. Believing that "an average
congregation is unable to sustain its attention throughout a
verse-by-verse exposition of a passage of scripture," D. W.
Cleverley Ford recommended focusing on a single verse and
using a theme suggested by this verse.[8]

A Clause, a   Finally, it is possible to use a clause, a
Phrase, or a Word   phrase, or a word as a text. The limitations and hazards are obvious, but occasionally a striking
and quite biblical sermon can leap from just one word. The
multivolume *Theological Dictionary of the New Testament*,
edited by Gerhard Kittel, and its Old Testament counterpart
lay the riches of single words at the preacher's feet. Consider
the possibilities of such a word as *aiōnios*, "eternal;" or
doulos, "slave;" or *kairos*, "time" ("opportune" time). Paul

35

Tillich often took only one word from a text and built his entire sermon around that word, but for that very reason his sermons sometimes missed the context or emphasis of the biblical author.

Preference for The length of the chosen text often deter-
Longer Texts mines the amount of variety it offers. A short text furnishes the minister with a point of departure, but a long text often provides the hills, the valleys, and the broad fields for the entire journey—including the destination. Adam Clarke's wise counsel was this: "Seldom take a *very short* text; because a short one may not afford you sufficient matter to entertain and instruct your congregation."[9]

III. OBJECTIONS TO TEXTS

Strong It would seem that the very nature of the
Arguments preacher's task would settle the issue of whether to preach from a text. But this is not so! Some persons argue strongly that a minister should not confine himself to biblical texts.[10] And they are not altogether wrong. These are some of the arguments:

- The average minister does not have enough time to do the thorough research required to preach worthily on biblical texts.
- The person living today is not interested in what went on centuries ago; he wants to know how to live now.
- If the minister takes the text seriously some things will go unsaid: he cannot pursue some significant ideas and sentiments; he cannot hope to achieve the highest homiletical form.
- The view of truth presented in a particular text may be one-sided, and the minister cannot preach a full-orbed doctrine if he sticks to his text.

- The ideas in some texts, such as the imprecatory psalms, are sub-Christian. If these ideas are presented exactly as they stand, they will contradict clear teachings found in other parts of the Bible, particularly the New Testament.
- The thought forms of some texts belong to a bygone generation, and the present-day minister cannot hope to communicate with our sophisticated moderns in an obsolete language.
- The use of texts encourages the proof-text method of biblical interpretation, and the Bible as a whole can be saved only by sacrificing attention to its parts.
- Scholarly opinion is divided on the interpretation of many texts.

If these objections are valid, then it would seem that the only way in which the minister can give a positive message that has his complete confidence is to avoid the use of texts.

IV. DEFENSE OF TEXTS

Surmounting the Obstacles Some of the arguments against using texts are formidable and cannot be easily dismissed. But there are many ways through or around these barriers short of eliminating the text. Granted, all worthy preaching demands careful study of the text; there is no substitute for hard work. But the other problems do not have to be so arduous. Why does textual preaching have to be dull and unimaginative? The sermons of Helmut Thielicke and Walter Lüthi are filled with drama and vitality. Why must textual preaching be false when it presents fragments of the truth? We have received Christian truth piecemeal from our childhood, and we do not need a compendium of Christian doctrine in every sermon we hear. Why does textual preaching have to be irrelevant? Most texts can be interpreted in the light of present need; they can be translated into the speech of today; they can be understood in historical perspective from the point of view of mankind's progressive understanding of revelation. Why does textual preaching have to promote the proof-text method of interpretation? If the true meaning of the text is taken into account, there is little danger. Why does textual preaching have to be unsure and weakly apologetic? The meaning of most texts is passably clear, and these exist in abundance.

A Portable When the minister interprets the Bible well, it
Possession becomes the possession of the hearer; it is really his. Until one sees himself in its pages, it is just another book. But when he links every biblical event and teaching with his own day-to-day living, with his failures and successes, with his despairs and hopes, with his misery and happiness, the Bible truly comes to belong to him. He will not be at a loss when he reads it for himself. He can thread his way through its difficulties and never lose sight of its central purpose. He can go to it for his own edification, or he can impart its message to others. The members of the average congregation are like the Ethiopian official who as he read Isaiah the prophet was asked, "Do you understand what you are reading?" and answered, "How can I, unless someone guides me?" (Acts 8:30-31 RSV) Those who have a guide are fortunate: a knowledge of the Bible can open a new world to them.

NOTES

1. Karl Barth, *The Preaching of the Gospel*, trans. B. E. Hooke (Philadelphia: The Westminster Press, 1963), p. 28.

2. Bruce A. Rosenberg, *The Art of the American Folk Preacher* (New York: Oxford University Press, 1970), pp. 186–94.

3. Dwight E. Stevenson, *Preaching on the Books of the Old Testament* (New York: Harper & Brothers, 1961), pp. 15, 45, 164, 181; *Preaching on the Books of the New Testament* (New York: Harper & Brothers, 1956), pp. 39, 80, 198, 251.

4. See the excellent discussion by Charles E. Faw, *A Guide to Biblical Preaching* (Nashville: Broadman Press, 1962), pp. 73–95.

5. Harry Emerson Fosdick, *The Hope of the World* (New York: Harper & Brothers, 1933), pp. 145–55.

6. Cf. Andrew W. Blackwood, *Preaching from the Bible* (New York: Abingdon-Cokesbury Press, 1941), pp. 94–110.

7. Richard Francis Weymouth, trans., *The New Testament in Modern Speech* (5th ed.; Boston: The Pilgrim Press, 1939), pp. 387–90.

8. D. W. Cleverley Ford, *An Expository Preacher's Notebook* (New York: Harper & Brothers, 1960), p. 18.

9. Adam Clarke *et al.*, *The Preacher's Manual* (New York: T. Mason and G. Lane, 1837), p. 88.

10. Cf. John A. Broadus, *On the Preparation and Delivery of Sermons*, ed. Jesse Burton Weatherspoon (New York: Harper & Brothers, 1944), pp. 16-18.

CHAPTER THREE

MINING THE SCRIPTURAL TREASURES

Where is my next sermon coming from? This is the preacher's most frequently recurring anxiety. Sunday rolls around with paralyzing inevitability. When you have to preach not just one, but two, sermons the problem is intensified. A bright theological student at Princeton Theological Seminary, who had never had a pastorate, saw this situation looming up before him and expressed to me his doubts about entering the pastoral ministry. Brighter than the average student, loaded with personality, and remarkably able to complete a project, he nonetheless felt that he could not produce a new sermon each week.

To a degree, this may be your problem. What can be done about it?

I. PREPARING FOR THE FUTURE

Two Mistakes — The preacher can make two mistakes: (1) he can depend on last-minute desperation for the impetus needed to bring a sermon to birth, so that when the inspiration does not arrive on time or in sufficient quantity he becomes more and more fearful of his ability to meet the weekly homiletical demands; or (2) he can imagine that his one hundredth sermon will have to be as hard to get up as his first.

The Illusion of "Inspiration" — As for the first error, Saturday night is too late to be looking for a text and ideas for the next day. Henry Ward Beecher, one of the most popular and provocative clergymen of the nineteenth century, a superb pulpit orator, was known to choose his text regularly on Sunday morning. What writing was done on his sermon he did between the time he settled on his text and the moment the church bell rang, and he produced many great sermons with this technique. But he had a secret—he always kept several sermons in the process of preparation. When Sunday morning arrived he simply plucked the sermon that was ripest and most appropriate.

Preaching from the Overflow   Few great sermons will be preached with only last-minute preparation. The best sermons come from the overflow—from the abundance of deep living and patient accumulation of unhurried thinking. Phillips Brooks said,

> I think that the less of special preparation that is needed for a sermon, the better the sermon is. The best sermon would be that whose thoughts, though carefully arranged, and lighted up with every illustration that could make them clearer for this special appearance, were all old thoughts, familiar to the preacher's mind, long a part of his experience. [1]

This approach to sermon-making, given time, will correct the second mistake, that of our theological student who assumed that a new sermon must be built from the ground up each time it is needed.

Finding Texts   Take advantage of every opportunity to make notes of texts for use in your sermons. Many of them will come incidentally from your devotional reading of the Bible. Some persons would say that to look for sermons while doing your devotions is inimical, even deadly, to the best use of one's private worship. But is the minister ever isolated from his preaching task? Every private thought has social implications. What better way is there to read the Bible than to read

41

it with the freedom to consider its fullest implications? Therefore, make notes as you read, put them aside, evaluate them later, and add to them as you have opportunity.

A more systematic method will perhaps generate better results. *Consider this* helpful suggestion by Joseph R. Sizoo:

> For many years, indeed as long as I was the minister of a parish church, I observed a custom which became a sort of ritual with me. In the summertime when we go to the country, I rise rather early and sit alone either in the morning sun or before the fireplace with my King James Version. I also have with me the translations of Moffatt, Weymouth, and Goodspeed. I then begin by selecting some book. I read very slowly and creatively until some word or text strikes me full in the face. Then I stop my reading and put it down in a loose-leaf notebook at my side. It may be a word or an idea which has suggested itself in some fashion. I put down every thought which comes to me in that quiet period of reading. If during the day this idea unfolds, I put it down before the day is over. The next morning I begin reading where I left off and follow the same procedure. By the end of the summer I have, therefore, ample material on which I can creatively work and use as my backlog for months to come. I keep on working in this loose-leaf notebook constantly.[2]

The Option of   Other options are open, such as the use of a
a Lectionary   lectionary, that is, "an ordered system of selected readings" that have been selected for use in public worship throughout the church year. Although this system goes back to the synagogue in concept, it evolved only gradually into its present form. For centuries it has been used by Roman Catholics, Anglicans, and Lutherans, among others. These communions have used series of lessons from the Gospels and the Epistles which are virtually identical and derive from the work of Alcuin (A.D. 735–804).[3] Other lectionaries have appeared recently, such as the two-year series by the Joint Liturgical Group (1966) and the three-year series shared by the Protestant Episcopal Church, the Roman

Catholic Church, the United Church of Christ, and the Lutheran and Presbyterian Churches, among others.[4]

These recent lectionaries offer three lessons for each Sunday, thus giving considerable range of choice. (See Appendix C.) Professor Paul Scherer, for many years a parish minister, commended the use of lectionaries (or, the pericopes). He said that he had always used them and that he had never felt them to be a restriction.[5]

In my new pastorate after seminary, I discovered the value of a lectionary. Partly to take the pain out of getting a text for at least one sermon each Sunday and partly as a discipline to compel myself to come to grips with certain scripture that I might otherwise unconsciously avoid, I turned to lectionaries for help. I had long since been convinced in theory by Andrew Blackwood's counsel in his *Planning a Year's Pulpit Work,* but now I could see for myself what following the lessons for the Christian Year might offer. I was not disappointed. Neither were the members of my congregation. My sermons were better prepared because I had more time to ponder the modern relevance of the texts, as well as to dig out their ancient meaning. This did not become my exclusive method, yet I used it often enough and long enough to prove its value.

Lectio Continua   Another option is the method of preaching through Bible books or through certain sections of books. For example, you might preach a series on Genesis 1–11, as Helmut Thielicke did, or on the Gospel of John, as Walter Lüthi did. If you prefer shorter texts, a series on the Ten Commandments, the Beatitudes, or the Lord's Prayer has possibilities. It is inadvisable to undertake a long series of sermons on a Bible book before you have had successful experience with preaching isolated sermons on long passages. However, when you are ready for it, preaching through a book will richly reward both you and your people.

"I did that often in my parish ministry," said Eduard Schweizer. "I would interrupt the series and preach on a Psalm, if I wished, and then return to the series. If the text does not speak to you, omit it—after trying hard to listen to its message. Or, choose a longer paragraph without preaching on some difficult verses within it. Or, take just a section of a book of the Bible and preach through that. Be free!"[6]

Consider these additional suggestions:

1. Vary your preaching between Old Testament and New Testament books. Or, use regularly the other text (or texts) for the lection and include some reference to it in your sermon.
2. Study the entire book thoroughly before you begin a series on it.
3. Introduce the book to your congregation with a sermon highlighting the leading theme or themes.
4. Be aware that the leading themes of a book, particularly a Pauline Epistle, may appear in the early chapters. Therefore, do not make the mistake of prematurely giving them exhaustive treatment.
5. If certain paragraphs in a book do not have a timely message, omit them and go on to a passage that does speak relevantly.
6. On the other hand, do not overlook the remote or ultimate relevance of a text that has no immediate application.

In the sixteenth century, Martin Luther and John Calvin poured the treasures of evangelical truth into the hearts of their people by preaching through book after book of the Bible. Such an approach to sermon-making may not produce the most "popular" preaching, but it will produce the most solid results.

An Eclectic   A final option is to design your own preaching
Program   program, which may include features of the
other options. Such an approach has two significant
requirements—advance planning and periodic review. One
pastor I know planned his preaching in this way for more
than twenty years. He made a list of the needs of his
congregation, as he understood them, trying to be as
objective as possible. He noted their continuing needs and
their special needs. On this basis, he selected themes and
texts. This brought to his task the sense of large design and
pointed relevance. For the preacher, this was an exciting
opportunity for meaningful preaching; for the congregation,
it was an enriching pilgrimage.

In a lecture to a conference of Southern Baptist pastors,
Raymond Bryan Brown made a strong case for what he called
a "Biblical Year," a calendar of preaching and worship based
on the Bible. He has suggested the following calendar, to be
filled in as the preacher chooses with appropriate texts:

I. SEASON OF REVELATION IN THE OLD TESTAMENT
September, October, November
*Emphasis on patriarchs, Moses, prophets, Creation, Providence,
Covenant, etc.*
II. SEASON OF PREPARATION FOR THE ADVENT OF
CHRIST
December
*Emphasis on Old Testament prophecies, John the Baptist,
"fullness of time"*
III. SEASON OF THE LIFE AND TEACHINGS OF CHRIST
January, February
*Emphasis on great events: Sermon on Mount, parables, miracles,
healings, etc.*
IV. SEASON OF PREPARATION FOR EASTER
March
*Emphasis on self-examination, repentance, prayer, reconcilia-
tion, renewal, cross*

V. SEASON OF EASTER
April, May
The risen Christ; the cosmic Christ in Acts and Epistles

VI. SEASON OF PENTECOST
June
Seven weeks after Easter. Emphasis on Holy Spirit, inner life translated into outer witness

VII. SEASON OF THE LIFE AND DEEDS OF THE CHURCH
June, July, August
Doctrine of the church: fellowship, ordinances, beliefs, etc.; practical application of faith to the problems of everyday life[7]

Keeping Texts and Ideas and Finding Them Again

A practical problem arises for the preacher when he begins to accumulate texts and other sermonic material. How will he keep and find these treasures again? Settling upon and consistently using a simple filing system is an imperative economy for anyone who writes or speaks. Hours of valuable time can be saved when you know where to put your hands immediately on your materials. The simplest method I know is one suggested to me by Paul Scherer. I once asked him what kind of filing system he would recommend to a young preacher. "I'll tell you what I do," he said. "I get a large loose-leaf notebook and write or paste in what I want to keep. I read through it occasionally to appropriate what is there, and when I am preparing a sermon I have my illustrations."[8] You may wish to go a step beyond Dr. Scherer's suggestion and index this material by subject, thus making it more readily available. Another simple method, one recommended by Robert McCracken, utilizes a large spiral notebook divided into sections: a section for texts, a section for themes, and a section or two for illustrations. The text or theme should be entered on the left page as the notebook lies open, together with references to books and relevant scripture passages, jottings of any thoughts that the preacher has on text or theme, and tentative outlines. Illustrations in the last section of the notebook should be numbered, so that they can be easily keyed into the note pages in the first two sections.[9] Still another simple method makes use of manila folders on which texts and themes for a planned program are written. As the preacher reads and meditates, he drops into the appropriate folder the fruits of his work, gradually accumulating a mass of material that he can select from when moving into the last stages of sermon-making.

One final suggestion on filing: carry with you slips of paper on which to write wherever you are. In this way you can be spared the sin of fretting and frittering away your time while you wait for a plane or a friend. On February 21, 1963, I met Elton Trueblood at the Union Station in Louisville. His train was two hours and twenty minutes late. As I drove him to a speaking engagement, I asked him, "Are you able to do your daily writing stint with all of these speaking engagements?" (He had had sixty-three of them since January 1!) "Yes," he replied, "I just use all the time there is. I worked on the train all morning. I looked around, and I was the only person on the train working. Many of the others were fretting and complaining because the train was two hours late. What I dropped in the mailbox a few minutes ago were the twelve handwritten letters I wrote on the train. Complaint is the most unproductive of all human activities."[10] A day or so later, speaking to a group of seminarians, Trueblood said that he always carried with him slips of paper on which to make notes and that as he drove along in his car he would often stop beside the road and write something down.

David Rockefeller, president of the Chase Manhattan Bank, referring to those who have learned the practical uses of uncommitted time, said, "The eye of the painter is ever alert to form and color. The sculptor looks for shape and

47

contour in all about him. The dancer notes the gracefulness of a bird in flight, while the writer picks up and stores the little nuances of speech to which he is exposed."[11] To Rockefeller's statement we might add, the biblical preacher is forever on the lookout for some example or analogy to clarify or impress a text, and he captures and keeps his serendipitous discoveries, as well as his more pedestrian findings.

It is most important to get down the germ idea and as much of its development as you have time to write. You can lose dozens of good sermons and hundreds of choice illustrations by neglecting to make immediate notes. Take heed from the story of the man who got a sudden flash of inspiration so brilliant that he went into the garden to thank God for it and rose from his knees only to discover that he had completely forgotten it.

II. "EXCAVATING" THE TEXT

Putting Questions to the Text — The next step after the choice of a text is the homiletical exegesis. This involves putting a series of questions to the text in the privacy of the study. James Black called it "boxing the ears of the text,"[12] though I believe that his phrase suggests a kind of manhandling of the text, when what is needed is to surrender to the object of the text.

Inquiry as a means of exploiting the riches of a text can be quite useful if the text has been arbitrarily chosen, that is, chosen without reference to its immediately speaking to the one who will preach from it. I do not offer these questions as a *sine qua non* for sermon preparation. They are only a handy collection of tools for digging, but they will often turn up unexpected treasures. Before you have asked all of the questions in the following series, the vitality of the text and its possibilities for preaching should begin to be obvious.

Look with me at the text of Mark 1:16-20 (RSV) and then at the questions as they penetrate the text and work their way into the life situation of the preacher and the congregation.

And passing along by the Sea of Galilee, he saw Simon and Andrew the brother of Simon casting a net in the sea; for they were fishermen. And Jesus said to them, "Follow me and I will make you become fishers of men." And immediately they left their nets and followed him. And going on a little farther, he saw James the son of Zeb'edee and John his brother, who were in their boat mending the nets. And immediately he called them; and they left their father Zeb'edee in the boat with the hired servants, and followed him.

1. *WHAT IS THE TEXT ABOUT? Give the text a general theme from systematic theology, e.g., eschatology, worship, doctrine of God.*

In this case the theme might be the Christian mission or, perhaps, discipleship.

2. *WHAT DOES THE TEXT MEAN TO YOU? This question may seem premature. Should we not do careful exegesis and look at the history of the interpretation of the text first? Not necessarily. Your first impression is likely to be the understanding of the average reader of the text also. So it is a good place to begin. If further investigation shows that the facts will not bear out your first impressions, you are none the worse for it. We learn by contrast as well as by comparison. Besides, you will be aware of the average man's interpretation and can work from there. For example, consider "Blessed are the meek" and the like.*

By going with Jesus Christ, one finds himself or herself a part of the greatest enterprise on earth.

3. *WHAT CRUCIAL EXEGETICAL ISSUES IN THE TEXT MIGHT BEAR ON A CORRECT INTERPRETATION? A first impression of a text used to be enough to satisfy a congregation, whether the interpretation was correct or not. And, of course, God did not go out of business when his messengers could not read*

Hebrew and Greek or did not have access to scholarly commentaries. But people demand and deserve more of their ministers today.

A. M. Hunter: "Jesus has just proclaimed the advent of the Reign of God. His next step is to call four Galilean fishermen to be his disciples. For God's Rule does not operate in a void—it implies a people living under it." [13]

Eduard Schweizer: "Apparently Mark has added this story in an effort to show in a concrete way what such a new commitment could mean." [14]

The *Jerome Biblical Commentary:* "Although the words suggest an almost casual encounter, the vbs. *paragein* and *parerchesthai* (to pass by), when predicated of Jesus in the Gospels, occur in epiphanic stories." [15] See, for example, Matthew 9:27 and Matthew 20:30.

4. WHAT IS THE SIGNIFICANCE OF THE TEXT IN RELATION TO JESUS CHRIST AND THE HISTORY OF REDEMPTION? This applies to both Old Testament and New Testament texts. Gerhard von Rad wrote: "Wherever one of God's dealings with his people, or with an individual, is witnessed to, the possibility exists of seeing in this a shadow of the New Testament revelation of Christ. The number of Old Testament types is unlimited." [16] Moreover, the ethical teachings of Jesus and the apostles have to be seen as a part of and not apart from the movement of God's grace toward us and toward all men in the Christ event. Christian preaching is always within the context of God's purpose as revealed in Jesus Christ. This is quite clear in certain New Testament texts, e.g., John 3:16. But it is not so clear in relation to a text like Deuteronomy 6:5 (cf. Mark 12:30), where we are commanded to "love the Lord thy God with all thy heart."

Schweizer has noted: "It is important to see that in this text (twice!) as in Mark 2:14, *Jesus comes to them* (they are *not* part of the 'churchgoing people' of verses 14-15!). Jesus 'sees' them (as God 'sees' David before electing him as king!), before they realize what is happening. Jesus speaks to them and Jesus will make them fishers of men—so that they follow as if it went without saying."[17]

The expansion of the rule of God requires men and women committed to it and to God's purposes. The need is not primarily for unusually gifted people, but for extraordinarily dedicated people. It may demand, as in the case of Simon and Andrew, the giving up of a profitable occupation; or, as in the case of James and John, the eventual severing of family ties. The rule of God is present in the person of Jesus Christ, who says, "Follow me." Who can tell where it will lead and what it will cost?

5. WHAT HAS THE TEXT MEANT TO OTHER INTERPRETERS? This question points to such interpreters as Augustine, Chrysostom, Luther, Calvin, and Barth. Though the contexts of their interpretations were different in some respects from our own, their insights can enrich our present understanding of the text. The older interpreters were not so well equipped for a scientific study of the text as we may be in the twentieth century, but they were well equipped to expose the spiritual depth of the text. Protestants have rightly never felt bound by the interpretations of "the Fathers," but they have too often wrongly ignored them.

John Calvin, in *Institutes of the Christian Religion,* wrote: "Each man will bear and swallow the discomforts, vexations, weariness, and anxieties in his way of life, when he has been persuaded that the burden was laid upon him by God. From this will arise also a singular consolation: that no task will be so sordid and base, provided you obey your calling in it, that it will not shine and be reckoned very precious in God's sight."[18]

Matthew Henry: "The instruments Christ chose to employ in setting up his kingdom, were the *weak* and *foolish things of*

51

the world; not called from the great sanhedrim, or the schools of the rabbin, but picked up from among the tarpaulins *by the sea-side, that the excellency of the power* might appear to be wholly *of God,* and not at all of them. . . . We must sit loose to the world, and forsake every thing that is inconsistent with our duty to Christ, and that cannot be kept without prejudice to our souls."[19]

6. *WHAT IS THE POINT OF IMMEDIACY? WHERE DOES THE TEXT STRIKE CLOSEST HOME IN YOUR LIFE? The point of immediacy could be at one place one time and at another place another time.*

"Follow me." These words have unusual challenge now. The dangerous frontier today is not the foreign mission field, but the haunts of poverty, crime, injustice, and anarchy. However, this may be simply an invitation to begin something with Jesus, with no intimation at this point of hardships and difficulties to come. The disciples could have gone back home again the same evening—everything was still open. "Follow me," implies first only a few miles of common wandering.[20]

7. *WHAT IS THERE IN THE TEXT THAT WOULD MAKE IT DIFFICULT TO COMMUNICATE? What makes it difficult for you to accept it? You can anticipate some of the problems of your hearers as you honestly face your own. In addition, some of your hearers may have other problems. Here a bit of spiritual "clairvoyance" is called for.*

It is hard to believe that four mature, responsible men would give up their life's work on such short notice to be disciples of a man they had just met. In answer, we may see this as a highly condensed account of all that took place between Jesus and Simon and Andrew, and James and John. Also, we might consider the possibility of an earlier meeting, like that which John reports in his Gospel (John 1:35-42). It is more likely, however, that there is a purpose behind reporting that the disciples had no time for reflection on Jesus' call and immediately responded. "So it is that God's grace operates without the necessity of deliberation. As a result, discipleship is neither an individual ethical decision nor a thoughtful acceptance of propositions; yet in a very substantial way it is a new manner of acting and thinking which is sustained by the event of grace."[21]

8. CAN THE TRUTH IN THE TEXT STAND ALONE, OR DOES IT NEED TO BE SEEN IN RELATION TO A COUN-TERBALANCING TRUTH? The preacher does not have to offer a complete compendium of Christian truth each time he speaks. Nor must every one-sided thesis be brought into synthesis with its antithesis. But often the latter is helpful, perhaps even essential. Nevertheless, "a too well balanced sermon does not really convey its message." [22]

Everyday work is important. Someone has to work to support Jesus' followers and their families. Paul admonished, "If any one will not work, let him not eat" (II Thess. 3:10 RSV). Also, "If any one does not provide for his relatives, and especially for his own family, he has disowned the faith and is worse than an unbeliever" (I Tim. 5:8 RSV). The apostle worked as a tentmaker to support himself, but he enunciated the principle that the faithful teacher or preacher is worthy of the support of those he serves (I Cor. 9:9-12; I Tim. 5:17-18; cf. also, Luke 10:7). Foreign missionaries face unusual difficulties in rearing and educating their children. Unmarried priests often live their lives of obedience in unfulfilled loneliness. Can a missionary in good conscience sacrifice his children's future stability and happiness while he pursues his own calling? Should a man leave the emotional part of his life unfulfilled in order to serve God more single-mindedly? These questions have no simple answer. Yet it is clear: the world is richer because some persons have denied themselves and have had the willing comradeship of their families in their commitment.

9. WHAT ARE SOME OF THE CAUSES OF THE CONDITION OR SITUATION DISCUSSED OR SUGGESTED IN THE TEXT? The most interesting sermons ordinarily are those whose relevance is unmistakable—they deal with a present problem or difficulty. Just as it is often helpful to know the cause of a disease in order to treat it successfully, so it may be helpful to recognize the etiology of a need in the course of prescribing a remedy. Also, when you recognize the causes of an ordinary human situation not necessarily sinful or unpleasant in itself, this may point toward the need for a higher goal.

At first, Jesus' call to the disciples was open-ended. Nothing specific was demanded or guaranteed. He said, quite simply, "Follow me," though in the case of Andrew and Peter he went on to say, "I will make you become fishers of men." However, in Mark 2:4 and 2:20 the outcome of answering Jesus' call is not described. Eventually, the four disciples undertook new and more challenging tasks. Until they met Jesus, they were men occupied with work that they assumed they were born to do. For example, James and John followed their father Zebedee's line of work. What they did was necessary work. They helped provide for men's daily need for food. Until they met Jesus Christ and began to follow him, they were no doubt satisfied with their work, and they had a right to be so. The wishes of parents, the needs of the community, one's personal talents and inclinations, and the accidents of fortune make one what he is or lead one into his life's work. This is as it should be. But an encounter with Jesus Christ introduces a new element into the situation, and nothing can be quite the same again.

10. WHAT ARE THE THEOLOGICAL IMPLICATIONS OR PRACTICAL DUTIES THAT GROW OUT OF THE TRUTH OF THE TEXT?

Jesus had unusual authority. Otherwise, he would not have presumed to offer such a challenge to the fishermen. Futhermore, they recognized his unusual authority. Otherwise, they would hardly have left all and followed him.

Jesus manifested the electing grace of God. Jesus "saw" the fishermen. "He sees them as He later saw Levi, and this differentiating and electing seeing decides their fate according to the Evangelists, being followed at once by a call."[23]

The work of God in Jesus was not completed apart from the affirmative response of the fishermen.

God is at work in the world today as the name of Jesus Christ is pronounced over our lives through the church and its message of Good News. As the church disturbs our amiable complacency, setting before us the claims and challenge of Jesus Christ, we can be caught up in life's most exciting enterprise. This can happen in a shockingly disruptive experience, or it can happen in a gradually deepening and ever more demanding companionship with our Lord.

11. WHAT OBJECTIONS MAY BE RAISED TO YOUR CONCLUSIONS ABOUT THE IMPLICATIONS AND APPLICATIONS OF THE TRUTH OF THE TEXT? Anticipate emotional reactions and intellectual problems. Preaching that does its work cannot be taken for granted. Often the preacher can keep emotional reaction from becoming destructive. Moreover, he can often keep an intellectual problem from bogging down the sermon if he simply recognizes the existence of the problem and passes on to matters that both he and his hearers are more competent to deal with. It should be noted that the ancient rhetoricians made a place in a discourse for "answers to objections." [24] *It should be expected that the preacher, more than anyone else, should be warmly considerate and scrupulously fair.*

When one faces the demands of Jesus Christ that emerge from his gracious election and calling, he should not be criticized for saying something like this: "Surely this does not apply to everyone!" or "But is it fair? This might cause a complete upset of my whole life-style." Jesus Christ does not call all men and women to be missionaries or social workers, or to change occupations and leave home. He has a plan tailored for each person. The demands upon some are greater than those upon others, but each way has its own compensations. In truth, it is God's purpose to make each person's life different—radically different—but always better and more meaningful. Still, in fairness we have to admit that the difference is not always obvious. Those who do God's will in this world are not always rewarded here.

12. *WHAT WOULD BE THE RESULTS OF KNOWING OR FAILING TO KNOW, BELIEVING OR FAILING TO BELIEVE, OR DOING OR FAILING TO DO WHAT THE TEXT SUGGESTS? Considering the consequences of our decisions and actions is being realistic. Often our flagging wills need the extra boost of fear of punishment—not necessarily arbitrary punishment—or expectation of reward. This is not the highest or most desirable motivation, but it is a recognizable part of human experience. The Bible is not unwilling to give us the total picture.*

To go with Jesus Christ puts one in a position to do God's work among men. He goes forth "to preach the Good News to the poor," "to proclaim liberty to the captives, and recovery of sight to the blind, to set free the oppressed, to announce the year when the Lord will save his people!" (Luke 4:18-19 TEV.) To do something worthwhile for the poor, the handicapped, the persecuted, and all those who look to God for help—this should excite the imagination, challenge the will, and bring a sense of meaning to life that ordinary pursuits cannot give. To love actively is to love as God loves! Not to go with Jesus may result in missing these great opportunities.

13. WHAT MUST YOU DO TO MAKE THE MESSAGE OF THE TEXT REAL AND TRUE IN YOUR OWN LIFE? This is the point at which kerygma ("message") becomes martyrion ("witness"). The gospel becomes incarnate and is revealed through the preacher's own experience of it in the dimensions and configurations of his own need.

I must be willing to go where Jesus Christ would go—and in a real sense does go. I must not stay or go just where my love for security, for comfort, and for acceptance might dictate. To go with him always has an element of uncertainty, though one may go with the heartening certitude, "I know that as I go, I go with God, and he will never leave me or forsake me."

14. WHAT IS THERE IN GENERAL LITERATURE, IN BIBLICAL RESOURCES, IN PERSONAL COUNSELING, AND IN PERSONAL OBSERVATION AND EXPERIENCE THAT WILL EXEMPLIFY OR ILLUSTRATE THE TRUTH OF THE TEXT? The finest argument pales beside the strength of an actual instance of a truth. Moreover, human interest stories are endlessly fascinating.

George W. Truett was pastor of one of the world's largest congregations, a denominational statesman, and president of the Baptist World Alliance. As a young man, he had planned to become a lawyer. However, his church, which he had served as Sunday school superintendent, and for which he had often conducted services, decided that he should be ordained. Truett protested at first, pleading for time to decide, but the congregation was convinced that the time was ripe. Astonished, but finally submissive, he was ordained the day after he heard the church's proposal. Years later, Truett said, "If I had a thousand lives given me, and the Master should say, 'You wanted the first one to be a lawyer, but I wanted your first life to be that of a preacher; now you may make your own choice,' I would not hesitate one moment to give the whole thousand lives to Christ and His glorious gospel ministry."[25]

For Keith Miller, an official in an oil concern, going with Jesus Christ at first meant praying as he walked to and from the water cooler at work each day and then organizing an informal prayer meeting on the job. Eventually it led into writing, lecturing, counseling, and teaching, all of which activities have taken Miller via the printed page or in person into tens of thousands of homes and churches.[26]

John R. Sampey, while president of the Southern Baptist Theological Seminary, preached in many parts of the world, challenging young people with the words, "Give Christ Jesus all the keys of your life!"

I heard a man say as he looked back over his life with its many ups and downs, a life with Christ, "I wouldn't have had it any other way."

Tennessee Williams's aging actress, who kept herself going with drugs, oxygen, and sex, said with anxiety, "No mention of death, never a word on that odious subject."[27] The apostle Paul, on the other hand, could say, "To me to live is Christ, and to die is gain."

NOTES

1. Phillips Brooks, *On Preaching* (New York: The Seabury Press, 1964), p. 157.

2. Joseph R. Sizoo, *Preaching Unashamed* (New York: Abingdon-Cokesbury Press, 1949), p. 61.

3. J. G. Davies, ed., *A Dictionary of Liturgy and Worship* (New York: The Macmillan Co., 1972), pp. 211–12.

4. See Ronald C. D. Jasper, ed., *The Calendar and Lectionary* (New York: Oxford University Press, 1967) or Ernest A. Payne, Stephen F. Winward, and James W. Cox, eds., *Minister's Worship Manual* (New York: The World Publishing Co., 1969); and *Lectionary for Mass* (New York: Catholic Book Publishing Co., 1970) or *The Worshipbook—Services and Hymns* (Philadelphia: The Westminster Press, 1970).

5. Paul Scherer, *For We Have This Treasure* (New York: Harper & Brothers, 1944), p. 160.

6. Eduard Schweizer: personal communication; cf. original form of quote, *God's Inescapable Nearness*, trans. James W. Cox (Waco: Word Books, 1971) p. 16.

7. Raymond Bryan Brown, from suggestions in a lecture, copies of which were distributed to classes in The Southern Baptist Theological Seminary, Louisville, Kentucky.

8. Cf. Scherer, *We Have This Treasure*, pp. 147–55.

9. Cf. Robert J. McCracken, *The Making of the Sermon* (New York: Harper & Brothers, 1956), p. 90; also, Charles L. Rice, *Interpretation and Imagination* (Philadelphia: Fortress Press, 1970), pp. 103–5.

10. Elton Trueblood: personal communication.

11. David Rockefeller, "The Challenge of Leisure," *Vital Speeches*, April 1, 1964, p. 380.

12. James Black, *The Mystery of Preaching* (New York: Fleming H. Revell, 1924), pp. 92-93.

13. A. M. Hunter, *The Gospel According to St. Mark* (London: SCM Press, 1948), p. 31.

14. Eduard Schweizer, *The Good News According to Mark*, trans. Donald H. Madvig (Richmond: John Knox Press, 1970), p. 47.

15. Raymond E. Brown, Joseph A. Fitzmyer, and Ronald E. Murphy, eds., *The Jerome Biblical Commentary* (Englewood Cliffs: Prentice-Hall, 1968), 42:12:16.

16. Gerhard von Rad, "Typological Interpretation of the Old Testament," trans. by John Bright, *Essays on Old Testament Hermeneutics*, ed. Claus Westermann (Richmond: John Knox Press, 1963), p. 36.

17. Eduard Schweizer: personal communication.

18. John Calvin, *Institutes of the Christian Religion*, ed. John T. McNeill and trans. Ford Lewis Battles, (London: SCM Press, 1961), III, 10:6.

19. *Matthew Henry's Commentary on the Whole Bible* (New York: Fleming H. Revell [n.d.]), vol. 5, pp. 453-54.

20. Eduard Schweizer: personal communication.

21. Eduard Schweizer, *The Good News*, pp. 48–49.

22. Eduard Schweizer: personal communication.

23. Karl Barth, *Church Dogmatics* (Edinburgh: T. & T. Clark, 1962), vol. 4, Part 3 (2), p. 589.

24. Lane Cooper, ed. and trans., *The Rhetoric of Aristotle* (New York: Appleton-Century-Crofts, 1932), pp. 235-40; cf. Edward P. J. Corbett, *Classical Rhetoric for the Modern Student* (New York: Oxford University Press, 1965), pp. 297–302.

25. Powhatan W. James, *George W. Truett: A Biography* (Nashville: Broadman Press, 1939), pp. 46–50.

26. Keith Miller, *The Taste of New Wine* (Waco: Word Books, 1965), pp. 83–92, paperback edition.

27. Tennessee Williams, *Sweet Bird of Youth* (New York: New Directions Books, 1959), pp. 33–34.

CHAPTER FOUR

THE ANATOMY OF THE SERMON

Necessary Preliminaries The shape of the sermon and of its separate parts is what you are working toward. But certain factors determine that final shape and its content. Without attention to these important preliminary matters, your sermon will lack unity and precision of purpose. Also, the material you employ may not be appropriate even to such purpose as you have.

Idea and Purpose Before you put your sermon in final or even semifinal form, state your central, controlling idea in one brief, crisp sentence. Next, decide on the general controlling purpose, whether it is to explain that central idea, to convince the hearers of its truth, to use it to revitalize them in some area or areas of their lives, or to use it to challenge them to some definite, observable action.

Effective Control Your controlling purpose will do precisely what the adjective suggests: it will control the shape and content of the sermon. For example, a sermon to explain will require one type of illustration, and a sermon to revitalize will require a different type. Even the manner of delivery of a teaching sermon will differ from the manner of a persuasive sermon. Your controlling purpose makes the difference.

The Whole and Its Parts Aristotle noted that in dramatic tragedy there is always the division of beginning, middle, and end.[1] Writers on writing have insisted that aspiring authors give heed to Aristotle's simple observation and plot their stories accordingly. This applies also to sermons. Sermons need *introduction, body,* and *conclusion,* the standard and long-recognized main parts of a literary entity. Within each of these parts, of course, there is vast room for variety.

I. THE BEGINNING

The Importance of Beginning Well The importance of a good beginning for the sermon cannot be overemphasized. If you begin with a discussion of technical matters in the structure of the text or with some banal opening remarks before you get to what you really want to say, you may lose the audience before you have hardly begun. One preacher's invariable method of beginning his sermon was to announce his text and say, "This is a very significant verse." A member of his congregation remarked, "The verse may be significant, but why does he have to begin so insignificantly every time?"

Starting with the Text Often your text will be so striking that it would be a mistake to talk about anything but the text itself in the opening sentences. For instance, a preacher read his text from II Kings 8:13: "And Hazael said, But what, is thy servant a dog, that he should do this great thing?" The preacher paused, then said, "Dog or no dog, he did it!" Karl Barth rather consistently moved at once into his text, considering a formal introduction unnecessary, inasmuch as the entire service up to the time of the sermon serves as an introduction.[2] However, it was Barth's immediate discovery of the hearer in the text which made his method winsome. The text does not have to be striking or dramatic—if only the hearer sees that *he* is there, that it is about *him.*

In a probing essay, Harry Emerson Fosdick asked,

Who seriously supposes that . . . one in a hundred of the congregation cares, to start with, what Moses, Isaiah, Paul, or John meant in those special verses, or came to church deeply concerned about it? . . . Only the preacher proceeds still upon the idea that folk come to church desperately anxious to discover what happened to the Jebusites.[3]

Leading up to the Text We cannot assume a prior interest in the Bible. It is often wise to take your hearers by the hand and lead them from where they are to where you have been and where you want them to go. My own practice when using a short text has often been to introduce the text and the sermon at the same time. My opening remarks, then, are neither a reading of the text nor a direct discussion of it. I lead up to the text, read it or quote it, and plunge immediately into the sermon. This approach, I believe, takes into consideration psychological factors that govern the gaining of audience attention without sacrificing the biblical basis of the sermon. In some types of sermons for special audiences the text might come most appropriately in the last main point or even in the conclusion.

Some Striking Openings The following opening sentences touch the hearer at a variety of sensitive points. While most of them are not obviously related to a specific text, none of them is so unrelated to biblical concerns that it could not lead into a Bible text.

"Suppose you had just been saying Good-bye to someone whom you loved intensely." James S. Stewart)

"When Jesus spoke these words, He turned history upside down." (Stewart)

"My career as a minister began during World War I." (Ralph W. Sockman)

"Jung maintains that one of the primary needs of man is to feel secure." (Robert W. McCracken)

"Christianity began not with subscription to a creed but with attachment to a person." (McCracken)

"What I have to say today was suggested by a member of this congregation." (McCracken)

"This ancient and dim figure of Abraham leads a procession which in some measure we all join." (Halford E. Luccock)

"I am venturing to begin our thought at a strange place—the bedside of an invalid." (Luccock)

"Mark Twain once said, 'If I were a heathen, I would erect a statue to energy and fall down and worship it.'" (John S. Bonnell)

"Once more on Christmas Sunday morning we come to the church to celebrate the Christ. But which Christ?" (Harry Emerson Fosdick)

"Last week in a brief post-Easter vacation I did what I wanted to do for a long time and became a tourist in my own hometown." (Ernest T. Campbell)

"It wasn't the Bethlehem Hilton, to be sure, but whatever its name and size, the inn that failed to accommodate Joseph and Mary two thousand years ago is familiar to more people than the most widely advertised hotel in the world." (Campbell)

"'The Lord is at hand.' Is that true? Or isn't it a fact that he is far, far away from us?" (Eduard Schweizer)

"This story begins as it could begin with us too. It begins with the fact that Elijah is sick of everything—so fed up that he runs away." (Schweizer)

Charles Reynolds Brown, a great preacher and teacher of preachers, once said:

> In my own practice, while I never use a manuscript in preaching, there are five sentences in my sermon which I always write out in advance and know by heart—the first one and the last four. I like to begin, if I can, with a sentence as good as I know how to make it, so that the first ball may be pitched, if possible, right over the plate and at the proper level.[4]

<u>Writing the</u>   Some introductions should be written before
<u>Introduction</u>   the body of the sermon has been determined,
and some—perhaps most—after. If you begin with a problem
that you wish to explore and for which you attempt (with the
hard thinking of your audience) to find a solution, begin
working on the introduction. C. S. Lewis noted, "You find
out what the moral is by writing the story."[5] So it may be
with a particular sermon. First, state and illustrate the
problem; then, get hot on the trail of a solution. In other
types of sermons, you must know what you are going to
introduce before you attempt to introduce it. Therefore, the
introduction might be the last part of the sermon which you
prepare.

II. THE MIDDLE

Good structure determines good listening. For this reason,
time spent giving the main ideas of the sermon proper
sequence, balance, and unity is responsible stewardship.

<u>No Standard</u>   A sermon can have no meaningful design or
<u>Outline</u>   outline apart from a significant controlling idea
that can be simply and clearly stated. (In the homily or
narrative sermon the idea or ideas will be locked into the
structure of the text or of the events.) H. Grady Davis states
the case impressively:

> The master of his craft will do most of his work on the idea in its
> clear and simple structure, will ponder it long, will come back to it
> constantly, will search deeply for its true meaning and its divine
> and human import, will try its power on his own soul, knowing
> that any work he does apart from this basic idea is wasted.[6]

The useful outline, therefore, will grow out of the
controlling idea that emerges from the materials you have
gathered, as well as from your own meditation; and this
outline will be chastened by the result you hope to

65

accomplish in your hearers. This means that there is no standard outline that will provide a model for every sermon you need to preach. Some preachers bore their audiences to rebellion with sameness of approach. The hearers can always count on three points and a poem, and once the text is announced, they can predict with accuracy both outline and treatment before the preacher is through the introduction. What follows is intended to indicate and support a more excellent way.

EXPOSITORY SEQUENCES
FOR SERMONS DESIGNED TO EXPLAIN

The Homily As already noted (chap. 1), the homily is perhaps the simplest and oldest form of preaching. This verse-by-verse, phrase-by-phrase, or word-by-word discussion begins at the beginning of the text and usually proceeds straight on to the end.

This form of preaching can be done well only with the kind of text which has a true underlying unity that enables the preacher to move upward step by step to a significant level, rather than across only on a horizontal line of thought. As R. C. H. Lenski describes the homily:

> There is no theme with such strict control of the parts [as in the thematic sermon], and no strict pattern to which each part in its place must conform if the pattern is to be carried out symmetrically. Instead of strict symmetry there is free development. . . . We take the parts as they naturally come in the text. We attempt no coordination, which would be a logical control. We seek for no balance, no design or pattern in laying them out.[7]

Donald Macleod has rightly noted that the expression *"just a homily"* is both incorrect and unbecoming in that it suggests a sermon hurriedly thrown together with disjointed and hurried comments upon a scripture passage. He says:

> A homily presupposes (a) on the part of the congregation an intellectual and spiritual maturity much above average and (b) on the part of the preacher an unusual breadth of scriptural comprehension, the ability to be interesting, and a pastoral sensitivity which aids relevance.[8]

The sermons of Karl Barth and Eduard Schweizer are notable examples of sermons of the homily genre. What one thinks of as a homily is modified somewhat in these sermons, particularly Schweizer's. For Schweizer sometimes—when it is necessary to establish a bridge from the hearer to the text—begins at some distance from the text and moves toward it through a contemporary introduction. Moreover, when I was translating his titleless sermons for publication, I had no difficulty finding a unifying theme running through each of them which suggested a title that captured the theme.

One sermon by Schweizer, "God's Inescapable Nearness," has its thematic center of gravity in the sentence found squarely in the middle of the four-verse text, "The Lord is at hand" (Phil. 4:4-7). This becomes the unifying theme and key for interpretation of the first two verses and the last two verses. Schweizer then proceeds verse-by-verse through the four verses in the order in which they appear in the text, skipping, of course, "The Lord is at hand," since that is the theme with which he began.[9]

Barth's later sermons—those preached to the inmates of Basel prison—use short texts; however, they develop the same way as his earlier sermons with longer texts. The shorter texts do require more of the preacher in the way of detail. One of Barth's sermons is on Leviticus 26:12: "I will walk among you, and will be your God, and you shall be my people," and the text is discussed part-by-part as the parts appear:

I. "I will walk among you."
II. "And will be your God."
III. "And you shall be my people."
    "You"
    "My"
    "People" [10]

No abstract or summary presentation of the homily can do it justice, for the homily at its best is an organic unity and has to be examined in its totality in order to be properly understood and evaluated.

Expository Sermon   The expository sermon differs from the homily mainly in the fact that its structure is determined by two foci: (1) the central idea of the text, stated in the form of a theme or proposition; and (2) the controlling objective as determined by the preacher. One thinks of a text of several verses rather than of one verse, though length of text is not decisive. John A. Broadus said, "An expository discourse may be defined as one which is occupied mainly, or at any rate, very largely, with the exposition of Scripture." [11] Broadus asserts that two requisites are unity and an orderly structure. [12] This type of sermon often follows the sequence of verses or phrases in the text, but not of necessity. An outstanding example is a sermon on John 4:32-38, "Some Laws of Spiritual Work," by Broadus. In the introduction, the preacher describes the disciples' reaction when they returned to Jesus from the city to which they had gone for food. Then he makes a "contract" (as Ralph Nichols would term it) with his congregation: "Now, from this passage with its images, I have wished to discourse upon *some laws of spiritual work,* as here set forth. . . . What are the laws of spiritual work which the Savior here indicates? I name four: . . ." After this, Broadus proceeds with his sermon as follows:

I. Spiritual work is *refreshing* to soul and body. "My food is to do the will of him that sent me, and to accomplish his work."

   A. We all know the power of the mind over the body.

   B. The only way to learn to love spiritual work is to keep doing it.

II. There are *seasons* in the spiritual sphere. "Say not ye, There are yet four months, and then cometh the harvest? behold, I say unto you, Lift up your eyes and look on the fields; for they are white already to harvest."

   A. In the history of our faith, there are sowing seasons and reaping seasons.

   B. In individual churches, there are seasons of sowing and reaping.

   C. In our own individual souls, it is likewise true.

III. Spiritual work *links the workers in unity*. "Herein is the saying true, One soweth, and another reapeth. . . . Other men have labored, and ye are entered into their labors."

   A. It is true in the history of our faith . . . and of all the higher work of humanity.

   B. It is true of spiritual work—

      1. As we are linked with our contemporaries;

      2. As we are linked with the past;

      3. As we are members of an individual church;

      4. As we recognize our individual accountability and at the same time our close connection and interaction with one another.

IV. Spiritual work *has rich rewards*. "And he that reapeth receiveth wages, and gathereth fruit unto life eternal."

   A. Sometimes we try to do good and apparently, but not actually, fail.

   B. We can do good in very quiet ways.

C. We can do others, and therefore ourselves, more good than we know.

D. Spiritual work shall also be rewarded in the lord of the harvest's commendation and welcome.[13]

Narrative Sermon   A narrative sermon unfolds along the lines laid down in the biblical text. It may alternate between narrative detail and application; it may give a simple historical narration and then draw out the lessons; or it may tell the story in such a way that the application is implied.

Harry Emerson Fosdick briefly narrated the events of the life of Ezekiel, compared Ezekiel's time to the present, and drew out the lessons for his hearers, sometimes illustrating them from Ezekiel's life. His text, "The Spirit entered into me, and set me upon my feet," appears twice in Ezekiel (Ezek. 2:2; 3:24), and the words suggest the need for stamina. Fosdick asks, "What goes on in the life of a man who has it?" His sermon is the answer.

"How to Stand Up and Take It"

I. A man like Ezekiel certainly started by tackling himself.

II. He saw that a difficult situation can positively call out a man's powers.

III. He saw that when God made him, God had put into him some qualities that were meant for just such difficult occasions.

IV. Ezekiel believed that whatever happened, God was not dead.

V. This thing that happened to him was not so much something he did, as something that was done to him.[14]

An excellent method—and certainly in line with what many scholars believe was Jesus' method with his parables—is the third method mentioned above. Joseph Sittler indicated that some of his best preaching was done in this way. In preaching to university congregations, he would narrate a biblical incident or story, and just when some sophisticated hearer was likely saying to himself, "And now for the moral!" Sittler would end the sermon, leaving the thrust of the story itself to drive home the message.[15]

Extended passages, if not entire sermons, by Peter Marshall indicate how the application of a teaching by identification and by implication can take place. In the following passage, the hearer can feel himself a part of the multitude pushing and shoving toward Jesus for some gift or blessing:

> It is Jesus Whom they are crowding to see. They want to look on His face to see the quality of His expression that seems to promise so much to the weary and the heavy-laden; that look that seems to offer healing of mind and soul and body; forgiveness of sin; another chance—a beginning again.[16]

Allusions to contemporary persons, places, objects, and events can often make participation in the ancient story easier. In a sermon on Jesus' call of the disciples when by the Sea of Galilee, Eduard Schweizer says,

> In fact, they do not even know who this Jesus really is. But they are not totally ignorant. This is how they feel: "We are not here alone—just Andrew and Peter; our family; father and nets and business; our own little house down there on the seacoast; and every passing day the same as the day before." They know that God is real too. God is real, but not in the same way in which we might know that the constellation of the Great Bear is somewhere above us in the sky, though we do not know exactly where. They know that God is on the coast of the Sea of Galilee or at 34 Hoesch Lane.[17]

Concreteness such as that implicit in the narrative sermon is normal for black preaching and is an important key to its effectiveness. An outstanding black preacher told me during the days of the "Black Revolution" in the 1960s, "When I preach on the Exodus, I don't preach it as if it happened thousands of years ago. The Exodus is now—and I preach it that way."[18] That is, in truth, the only reason for preaching narrative sermons. We are there! When the hearer is made to feel that he is there, the given structure of events in the text provides the framework, the dramatic continuity, for the entire sermon—including conflict, crisis, and resolution.

THEMATIC SEQUENCES
FOR SERMONS DESIGNED TO EXPLAIN

In a thematic sequence, the theme itself, more than the text, controls the development of the sermon. The sermon will be faithful to the meaning of the text, but it will not be bound by the sequence of the ideas in the text. Sometimes theme development and text will coincide sequentially, so that no better arrangement of the ideas can be devised than that offered by the text itself.

Enumerative Outline The simplest thematic sequence is the enumerative outline. The preacher has several separate and distinct things to say on his theme, and he lists them one after the other. While the outline may sound like a laundry list because of its almost unrelated items, it can sometimes be the one best way to set forth the ramifications of a theme. Normally, five main points in a sermon constitute the outer limits beyond which the preacher ought not to go; however, theme or circumstances may justify breaking this rule. Consider this outline of a sermon on Galatians 5:22-23:

"The Marks of Sainthood"
I. Love
II. Joy

III. Peace
IV. Longsuffering
V. Kindness
VI. Goodness
VII. Faithfulness
VIII. Meekness
IX. Temperance

Each of the points in this "string of pearls" could well serve as a separate theme in a series of sermons. In fact, W. E. Sangster developed each of these words in separate chapters in his book *The Pure in Heart*. While the values of this type of sermon may be apparent, so are its weaknesses. Whether such a sermon is biblical or not does not depend entirely on one text; it may reflect an overarching biblical concern that comprehends many verses and chapters. The separate points may deal with one text or several.

Topical Outline A closely related type is the topical outline. The points in this outline are also discrete entities. They are related to each other only through the sermon theme. The distinctly topical outline has been highlighted by the words "jewel," "diamond," and "facet" in an effort to describe and characterize it. It looks at the sermonic theme from several angles and may have any number of points. The outline is produced by response to certain key words such as these: causes, results, conditions, occasions, purposes, means, comparisons, contrasts, forms, characteristics, reasons, examples, methods, elements, principles, uses, errors, proofs, weaknesses, meanings. It is often an answer to such questions as Why? How? When? and Where? James S. Stewart outlined a sermon on Hebrews 12:22-25 in this way:

"Why Go to Church?"
I. It is a spiritual fellowship.
II. It is a universal fellowship.

73

III. It is an immortal fellowship.
IV. It is a divine fellowship.
V. It is a redeeming fellowship. [19]

The variation of this type of outline that classifies or categorizes persons, places, or things will have a limited number of points. Either the text or the nature of the theme limits them. Halford E. Luccock noted:

> Many of Jesus' parables turn on some kind of classification: the talents, the sower, the good Samaritan, or those many twofold classifications which draw on the powerful effect of contrast—the prodigal and his brother, Pharisee and publican, wise and foolish virgins, sand and rock foundations. [20]

It is obvious that in a sermon on the persons in the Godhead, only three main parts of the body of the sermon are possible in the simple outline form: (I) God the Father, (II) God the Son, and (III) God the Holy Spirit. Compound forms or other types of outline may use categorizing. A striking example is a sermon by Sangster on John 1:42, "Jesus looked upon him, and said, Thou art Simon the Son of John: thou shalt be called 'Rock.'"

"Christ Has Double Vision"
I. Simon
   A. Simon as his friends saw him
   B. Simon as he saw himself
   C. Simon as Christ saw him
II. You
   A. You as your friends see you
   B. You as you see yourself
   C. You as Christ sees you [21]

Cumulative Narrative Outline   An interesting variety of explanatory sermon has been called the "cumulative narrative." To make a point and hammer it home the preacher tells a series of stories that exemplify or illustrate that point. C. Roy Angell wanted to give emphasis to the words of the apostle Paul, "For I reckon that the sufferings of this present time are not worthy to be compared with the glory which shall be revealed in us," and he did so by seizing upon a comparison between "hardships, disappointments and frustrations" and the diamond dust that is used to polish precious stones.

"Diamond Dust"

What does God use for diamond dust on you and me? I can readily think of three things.

  I. The compulsion of circumstances
     Story of shipwrecked apostle
     Story of ministerial student and President Coolidge
  II. Hardships
     Story of couple who adopted handicapped children
     Story of woman who directed schools for the blind
       and deaf
  III. Prayer
     Story of Norman Vincent Peale and businessman[22]

Explanation will occupy much of the preacher's pulpit time and effort. If he is a pastor, he has been assigned also the role of teacher. He will, of course, fulfill the need for several types of teaching, but his primary educational task is that of imparting the content of the Scriptures.

SEQUENCES FOR SERMONS
DESIGNED TO CONVINCE

We have biblical precedent for sermons that argue for the truth of God. Paul, the greatest of the apostles, used the best rabbinic logic to make a case. He was under no illusion that his arguments could embrace all of God and God's ways, yet he attempted to make his convictions and assertions as understandable and credible as possible. Only after he had done his best did he say, as we all must say at last:

> O depth of wealth, wisdom, and knowledge in God! How unsearchable his judgements, how untraceable his ways! Who knows the mind of the Lord? Who has been his counsellor? Who has ever made a gift to him, to receive a gift in return? Source, Guide, and Goal of all that is—to him be glory for ever! Amen. (Rom. 11:33-36 NEB)

Moreover, the apostle apparently went outside his usual rabbinic methods of disputation when a non-Jewish environment called for it. In Athens he argued with the Greek philosophers on their own grounds, so that his critics called him a "babbler," "a seed-picker," that is, a man who picks up odd bits of secondhand and undigested learning.[23] However, for his trouble, so we are told, "some men joined him and believed, among them Dionysius the Areopagite and a woman named Damaris and others with them" (Acts 17:34 RSV).

From the rhetoricians' viewpoint there are three modes of persuasion: (1) *logos*—"reason," (2) *pathos*—"feeling," and (3) *ethos*—"character."[24] None of these, so the theologians would say, is capable in and of itself of bringing one to a vital apprehension of truth as truth is understood in the Bible, that is, truth in encounter with the living God as revealed in Jesus Christ. Still, each of them plays a significant role. Reason is important not so much for its ability to overwhelm a reluctant intellectual rebel as for its ability to win the clarity an inquirer seeks, to give credibility to truths that have been shrouded in misunderstanding, and to lend recognition and respectability to views too easily ignored. The words of

Jesus, "He who has ears to hear, let him hear," often find fulfillment because someone who has ears to hear has been helped to hear through the efforts of a preacher who has given him every good reason to hear.

Thesis-Antithesis-Synthesis   One method of sermonic reasoning uses what is called the thesis-antithesis-synthesis sequence, which is modeled after a concept from G. W. F. Hegel's philosophy of history. Examples that antedate Hegel, however, can be found even as far back as St. Augustine. This is the method: first, a thesis is posited; second, a contradictory thesis is opposed to the first; third, the truth in each of these antithetical statements is brought together in a synthesis that is a higher expression of truth—and it is truth in interrelation.

A sermon taking its cue from Hegel's method might have Ephesians 2:8-10 for its text and be structured as follows:

"Getting in God's Good Graces"

How can we please God? What must we do or not do? What is God's role in the matter?

I. We may try the way of good works.
   A. It is a reasonable way.
   B. It leads to frustration.
   C. It is an inadequate way.
II. On the other hand, we may assume that God is pleased enough already.
   A. Three signs mark this way:
      1. "God expects little."
      2. "God is merciful—forget your sins."
      3. "The rules don't apply to you."
   B. These signs are misleading.
   C. It is an inadequate assumption.
III. However, God is pleased by those who trust him

77

completely and live out a right relationship with him through good works.

Extended Argument   Another logical sequence is simply a line of argument that lays down one reason after another for the truth of a central idea or proposition. Each step may be biblically oriented, or some of the steps may ground their credibility in, let us say, psychology or philosophy. In any case, the biblical concept will be ultimate and decisive. The sermons of James Stewart are not characteristically argumentative; however, one of his sermons in a series entitled "God and the Fact of Suffering" lays down three propositions for whose truth the preacher argues. The text is Hebrews 5:8 in Moffatt's translation: "Son though he was, he learned by all he suffered."

"Wearing the Thorns as a Crown"
I. It takes a world with trouble in it to make possible some of the finest qualities of life.
II. It takes a world with trouble in it to satisfy man's demand for a dangerous universe.
III. It takes a world with trouble in it to train men for their high calling as sons of God, and to carve upon the soul the lineaments of the face of Christ.[25]

Such objectives can, of course, be sought more formally by following this natural arrangement of ideas:

1. State the problem.
2. Arrange the evidence in order, first on main points, then on subordinate points.
3. Examine the credibility of the evidence.
4. State the possible implications of all evidence not totally rejected.

5. Weigh conflicting evidence in the scale of probability.
6. Give your verdict.[26]

Cooperative Sometimes it is necessary, in order to highlight
Techniques a biblical truth, to consider various interpretations one after the other and to exclude them one after the
other as the "real" truth is approached. The preacher will
attempt to be fair, retaining whatever truth may be in the
interpretation he excludes. This method has the advantage of
including the hearer, considering with him the problems and
deciding with him what to do about them. George A.
Buttrick's sermon in Harvard's Memorial Church on the
assertion of Psalm 24:1, "The earth is the Lord's," is a clear
example. Excluding one view after another as to the
ownership of the earth, Dr. Buttrick brings us to the
declaration of the text and the Christian implications of it.

"Who Owns the Earth?"
   I. Men have said in certain eras, "The earth is the
      devil's."
  II. In my time in college thoughtful men were saying,
      "The earth is the earth's."
 III. Our generation says flatly, "The earth is man's."
  IV. The earth proclaims its Divine Original, at least
      fitfully, even to our time-bound eyes. . . . "The earth
      is the Lord's."
   V. Here Dr. Buttrick shows how God in Jesus took bread
      and wine, things of earth, as well as the cross, and
      made sacraments of them.[27]

The idea or issue in the sermon may be approached
interrogatively, as in the following outline on the theme of
forgiveness. The texts are Ephesians 4:32 and Luke 7:36-50.

"Does Forgiveness Make Sense?"
I. Does forgiveness satisfy the requirements of justice?
II. Does forgiveness help the person forgiven?
III. Does forgiveness help the one who forgives?

Lewis and Nichols say of the interrogative pattern, "It has the advantage to the speaker of making him sound quite judicious, learned, and restrained."[28] Perhaps an added bonus for being convincing!

From Causes to Cures   In quest of solutions to vexing problems, it is often helpful to ferret out the cause or causes that give rise to the problems. A medical procedure involving diagnosis and prescription provides us with a model that can be divested of its medical terminology and used as often as needed. The following outline moves toward biblical solutions, which are found in the second part of the second main point below.

"The Causes and Cure of Talebearing"
I. Diagnosis
   A. Symptoms
      1. Faultfinding
      2. The raised eyebrow
      3. Slanderous remarks
   B. Causes
      1. Irritability
      2. Carelessness
      3. Insecurity, jealousy, and envy
II. Remedy
   A. Theory
      1. Patience
      2. Thoughtfulness
      3. Self-examination

B. Method of treatment
   1. Looking for the good (Phil. 4:8)
   2. Living by the golden rule (Luke 6:31)
   3. Conversion (I John 3:14)

Challenging   One of the most stirring sermons I heard from
an Axiom   my pastor during my high school days was a
rebuttal of a magazine article saying that the church was on
its way out. Such sermons do not appear regularly on the
preacher's homiletical agenda, but they are often needed.
Merrill R. Abbey has made a strong case for the need for
sermons that grapple with the contemporary mind. In his
Preaching to the Contemporary Mind, he uses a list of axioms
brought together by Emil Brunner to show how modern man
thinks, and he brings the truth of the gospel to bear on them.
His method is not one of angry polemic, but of intelligent
inquiry and hearty affirmation. In a sermon sketch he replies
to the axiom, "Beyond death nobody knows," using I
Corinthians 15:12-19:

"Robbing Death of Absurdity"

  I. To delete resurrection from faith's horizon you must
     begin by erasing it from history: "If there is no
     resurrection of the dead, then Christ has not been
     raised."
 II. To delete the resurrection you must excise it from
     experience: "If Christ has not been raised, your faith is
     futile and you are still in your sins."
III. To delete the resurrection you must begin over again
     in all your thinking about God: "We are found to be
     misrepresenting God, because we testified of God that
     he raised Christ, whom he did not raise if it is true that
     the dead are not raised."[29]

Being convinced of the truth of a matter is an important step in the process of making many vital decisions. However, if conviction does not precede a decision of faith, it will certainly be sought after the fact, as in St. Anselm's faith in search of understanding.

SEQUENCES FOR SERMONS DESIGNED TO MOTIVATE

If a sermon has understanding or belief as its immediate goal, the ultimate goal is, doubtless, motivation. However, some sermons are clearly designed to create some immediate inner or outward response. These sermons either reap a harvest from previous planting and watering, where other teachers or preachers have faithfully sowed and tended the word, or they plant, water, and harvest all in the same sermon. Phillips Brooks, in one of his famous Yale Lectures, said, "A sermon exists in and for its purpose. That purpose is the persuading and moving of men's souls."[30] Whether the persuading and moving takes place a year from now or this very hour, the goal is the same.

Sermons that motivate are of two general types: those that have to do mainly with inner feelings and attitudes and those that call for open, observable action. On the one hand there are sermons to inspire, encourage, and comfort; on the other hand, there are sermons to call to public decision, commitment, and action.

Different motives come into play and impel the hearer to feel or to act in certain ways. These motives arise from appeals to dynamic needs relating to (1) physiology, (2) safety, (3) love, (4) self-esteem, and (5) self-actualization.[31] The preacher should seek to recognize what makes or helps people do the things they do or what hinders them from doing those things. At the same time, he must beware of temptations to be false and unfair in his appeals.

One sermon pattern demonstrates the dynamics of motivation both of interest and of feeling and action. It parallels roughly the principles of salesmanship:

1. Get the prospective buyer's attention.
2. Help him to recognize some need that he has.
3. Show him what you have to meet that need.
4. Picture for him the advantages of acquiring what you have (or the disadvantages of not acquiring it).
5. Make the sale.

Clearly this method embodies the sermon from beginning to end; that is, it embraces introduction, body, and conclusion. As such, it has to be considered an organic whole.

Motivated Alan Monroe called his own method, which
Sequence employs the above steps, the *motivated sequence.*
This is defined as "the sequence of ideas which, by following the normal processes of human thinking, motivates an audience to respond to the speaker's purpose."[32]

Let me now strip this method of all but its barest essentials, demonstrating the five steps in an outline of a simple evangelistic sermon. The text is the well-known John 3:16.

"To Perish or to Live"

I. (Attention) Unless something is done for you, you will die spiritually.

II. (Need) You need to be infused with a new quality of life—"eternal life."

III. (Satisfaction) God will give you eternal life when you receive and obey his Son, Jesus Christ.

IV. (Visualization) If you refuse God's gift, you will remain in a state of death and dying. If you accept you will "pass from death to life" and come to know God and his Son in a new and fulfilling relationship.

V. (Action) Receive God's gracious offer now; identify yourself openly with Jesus Christ and with others who believe in him.

The motivated sequence is capable of many variations: the attention and need steps can be combined; need and satisfaction steps can be developed in parallel form when there are several aspects of need, each of which might require a specific means of satisfaction; satisfaction and visualization steps can also be treated the same way.

Some preachers have had their ministry revolutionized by discovering and following these five important steps. I heartily agree with Professor James Cleland on Alan Monroe: "His volume *Principles and Types of Speech* ought to be required reading for all preachers." [33]

COMBINATION SEQUENCES

It would be a mistake for a preacher to feel bound to certain predetermined forms for the sermon. One writer on the Elizabethan sermon said that the greatest preachers were those who were "found to be quite irregular in the construction of their sermons." [34] The preacher should be able to recognize different forms and be able to imitate them—for practice, at least. But knowing them, he should be free—free to use them or not use them, free to modify them or use them as they are, free to attempt new forms of his own making. One sermon outline may actually combine two or more basic forms. For example, the main points of the sermon body may be an enumerative outline, one of these points being developed with subpoints in the topical category, and, in turn, one of the subpoints being developed with sub-subpoints in the classification category. Remember: your central idea and your controlling objective properly determine the shape and details of your outline.

Plain Style Sermon The "plain style" sermon was widely preached in Stuart England, and was the predominant method of the Puritan clergy. This approach combined explanation, argument, and application. As it was sometimes used, explanation moved immediately to application, yielding to the urgency of the speaking occasion. This is how the plain style sermon might be constructed:

  I. Opening of the text (showing its meaning in the context and breaking it up into its separate parts)

 II. Proving any propositions drawn from the text (discussing their nature, truth, and reasonableness)

III. Making the application(s)[35]

As Gilbert Burnet, Lord Bishop of Sarum, explained in a book first published in 1692,

> This is, indeed, all that can truly be intended in preaching: to make some portions of Scripture to be rightly understood; to make those truths contained in them to be more fully apprehended; and then to lay the matter home to the consciences of the hearers, so directing all to some good and practical end.[36]

But of what use is this pattern now? It must be sharply modified to suit the needs of our day, though in overall concept it still has much to commend it. Consider this modification:

Introduction
  I. Exegesis or narration
 II. Exposition, interpretation, proof, or illustration (of the proposition(s) yielded by the exegesis or narration)
III. Application(s)
Conclusion

Perhaps no one has utilized this sermonic style more skillfully than James Cleland. Experience taught him that some contemporary congregations need an introduction to a discussion of a biblical text, for to plunge immediately into a text can lose interest that cannot be regained. Also, a conclusion—perhaps a story or some quoted lines—is often needed to pull the whole sermon together and give the application added force and effectiveness.

Cleland preached the following sermon in the chapel at Duke University. The text is the entire book of Jonah.

"Jonah—A Very Minor Prophet"

Introduction: There are two common and unsatisfactory approaches to Jonah—the humorous and the literal.

  I. Exegesis or narration (Key word: "Then") (A chapter-by-chapter summary and narration) "Jonah is a pamphlet written by a man with a large view of a great and merciful God. It anticipates the teaching of Jesus."

  II. Exposition or interpretation (Key word: "Always") (A development of the proposition yielded by the narration by chronological historical examples)

Proposition: "It is perfectly possible for a religious person to misunderstand the nature of God and to disagree with His ways with man."

Jonah misunderstood and disagreed.

So did the Pharisees toward Jesus.

So did the Church of Scotland toward McLeod Campbell.

"This is the kind of person God constantly has to work with."

  III. Application (Key word: "Now")

"There are [today] so many areas where Jonah is opposing God, and the Pharisees are opposing

Jesus, and the elect are opposing McLeod Campbell.
. . . Take the matter of Church membership, be it
across denominational lines or caste lines or class
lines. . . . That is what leads to change for the better:
a willingness to vote with God even when we
personally prefer no change. . . . *The Book of Jonah* is
a book for our times."

Conclusion: "Are we sorry that we are Jonahs? If not, are
we sorry for not being sorry that we are Jonahs? Yes?
Good. That gives God a chance to move in."[37]

It should be noted that a variation of this method might
develop two or more significant points in the same sermon.
If so, each of the points would be taken through each of the
three steps. However, to develop one significant point or
proposition well is probably best for most congregations.
Special audiences, such as a group of Bible scholars, may be
able to profit from a more detailed and compact sermon.

III. THE END

Importance of
the Conclusion Andrew W. Blackwood, a veteran preacher
and teacher of preachers, regarded the
conclusion as "the most important part of a sermon, except
for the text."[38] Yet many preachers give no attention to the
sermon's proper conclusion. They always make an evangelistic appeal, assuming that a clever modulation into the
stereotyped appeal will take the place of a carefully planned
conclusion.

Preaching has other objectives besides the evangelistic.
None of its objectives, including the evangelistic, must be
slighted. In the long run, it may be just as important to the
purposes of God for a husband and wife to decide to stay
together or for a businessman to decide to be a good steward
of his possessions, as for someone else to be persuaded to

make a profession of faith on a particular Sunday. In any case, you can give an evangelistic invitation after you have brought the sermon to its proper conclusion, perhaps following a brief prayer.

Cautions and Guidelines   The preacher should be cautious about the use of poetry in the conclusion. Often a brief poem is impressive. Quotations of stanzas of hymns can have telling effect. But, ordinarily, the use of other types of long poems will defeat the purposes of the conclusion.

The conclusion should be in line with the controlling objective of the sermon. Thus, it may be a summary of the sermon's main points or a restatement of its central idea. It may be an appeal for the hearer to act on the truth that has been presented. It may be an illustration that exemplifies and clinches the main point. At any rate, it must be carefully prepared, and the congregation should not be left in doubt as to what you have tried to accomplish.

NOTES

1. Aristotle, *De Poetica*, trans. Ingram Bywater, in Richard McKeon's (ed.) *Introduction to Aristotle* (New York: Random House, 1947), p. 634.

2. Karl Barth, *The Preaching of the Gospel*, trans. B. E. Hooke (Philadelphia: The Westminster Press, 1963), pp. 78–81.

3. Harry Emerson Fosdick, "What Is the Matter With Preaching?" in *Harry Emerson Fosdick's Art of Preaching: An Anthology*, ed. Lionel Crocker, (Springfield, Ill.: Charles C. Thomas, 1971), p. 30.

4. Charles Reynolds Brown, *The Art of Preaching* (New York: The Macmillan Co., 1922), p. 113.

5. Quoted by D. Bruce Lockerbie, *The Liberating Word: Art and the Mystery of the Gospel* (Grand Rapids: William B. Eerdmans Publishing Co., 1974), p. 16.

6. Henry Grady Davis, *Design for Preaching* (Philadelphia: Muhlenberg Press, 1958), p. 45.

7. R. C. H. Lenski, *The Sermon* (Privately published manuscript, n.d.), part 2, ch. 5.

8. Donald Macleod, "The Homily and the Sermon," *The New Pulpit Digest*, 55, no. 411 (January-February 1975), p. 14.

9. Eduard Schweizer, *God's Inescapable Nearness*, trans. James W. Cox (Waco: Word Books, 1971), pp. 93–98.

10. Karl Barth, *Deliverance to the Captives*, trans. Marguerite Wieser (New York: Harper & Brothers, 1961), pp. 60–66.

11. John A. Broadus, *On the Preparation and Delivery of Sermons*, ed. Jesse Burton Weatherspoon (New York: Harper & Brothers, 1944), p. 144.

12. *Ibid.*, p. 146.

13. John A. Broadus, *Sermons and Addresses* (Baltimore: H. M. Wharton and Co., 1886), pp. 26–44.

14. Harry Emerson Fosdick, *Living Under Tension* (New York: Harper & Brothers, 1941), pp. 92–101.

15. Joseph Sittler, in a lecture-discussion at the Southern Baptist Theological Seminary, Louisville, Kentucky, 1966.

16. Peter Marshall, *Mr. Jones, Meet the Master* (New York: Fleming H. Revell, 1950), p. 179.

17. Schweizer, *God's Inescapable Nearness*, pp. 35–36.

18. D. E. King: personal communication.

19. James S. Stewart, *The Wind of the Spirit* (London: Hodder & Stoughton, 1968), pp. 124–36.

20. Halford E. Luccock, *In the Minister's Workshop* (New York: Abingdon-Cokesbury Press, 1944), p. 139.

21. William E. Sangster, *Can I Know God?* (New York: Abingdon Press, 1960), pp. 35–42.

22. C. Roy Angell, *Iron Shoes* (Nashville: Broadman Press, 1953), pp. 44–45.

23. Cf. G. H. C. Macgregor, *The Acts of the Apostles,* "The Interpreter's Bible" (New York: Abingdon Press, 1954) 9:233.

24. Cf. Edward P. J. Corbett, *Classical Rhetoric for the Modern Student* (New York: Oxford University Press, 1965), p. 39.

25. James S. Stewart, *The Strong Name* (New York: Charles Scribner's Sons, 1941), pp. 147–58.

26. Cf. Robert Graves and Alan Hodge, *The Reader Over Your Shoulder* (New York: The Macmillan Co., 1961), p. 171.

27. George A. Buttrick, *Sermons Preached in a University Church* (New York: Abingdon Press, 1959), pp. 89–95.

28. Thomas R. Lewis and Ralph G. Nichols, *Speaking and Listening* (Dubuque, Iowa: William C. Brown Co., 1965), p. 95.

29. Merrill R. Abbey, *Preaching to the Contemporary Mind* (New York: Abingdon Press, 1963), pp. 170–72.

30. Phillips Brooks, *On Preaching* (New York: The Seabury Press, 1964), p. 110.

31. Raymond S. Ross, *Speech Communication* (Englewood Cliffs, N. J.: Prentice-Hall, 1965), p. 171.

32. Alan Monroe and Douglas Ehninger, *Principles and Types of Speech,* Sixth ed. (Glenview, Ill.: Scott, Foresman and Co., 1967), p. 265.

33. James T. Cleland, *Preaching to be Understood* (New York: Abingdon Press, 1965), p. 89.

34. Alan Fager Herr, *The Elizabethan Sermon* (New York: Octagon Books, 1969), p. 89.

35. Gilbert Burnet, *A Discourse of the Pastoral Care,* 16th ed. (London: William Tegg and Co., 1849), pp. 231-38.

36. *Ibid.,* pp. 231–32.

37. James T. Cleland, "Jonah—a Very Minor Prophet," in *Best Sermons,* G. Paul Butler, ed. (Princeton: D. Van Nostrand Co., 1962), pp. 280–85.

38. Andrew W. Blackwood, *The Preparation of Sermons* (London: Church Book Room Press, 1948), p. 177.

CHAPTER FIVE

STYLE AND ILLUSTRATION

"How can I get from my outline to the finished product?" This is the preacher's problem. He wants to know how to put flesh on the homiletical skeleton, how to expand a point or a sentence into a fully developed sequence of thought or paragraph.

Both form and content are involved. This should not be surprising, for it is difficult, if not impossible, to separate the two. We may not wish to say that the medium is the message, but we have to say, at least, that the medium is a significant part of the message. The form and modes of the early Christian message were inseparable from the substance of the Gospel. "*How* Jesus and his followers spoke and wrote," says Amos Wilder, "could not be separated from what they communicated."[1]

The personal equation in communicating the Gospel is unavoidable. As Phillips Brooks characterized it, preaching is "truth through personality." If this is true, then the kind of person the preacher is has major significance. The ancient rhetoricians recognized the primary importance of the speaker's *ethos* (his "character") in persuasion. No speaker, they believed, could hope to convince an audience and move it to action, unless he made it believe in his good sense and good will. This ethos would be reflected in the way he dramatized a story or an argument; for "style," as Buffon put it, "is the man himself."[2]

We must distinguish, then, between "style" and "styles." A man's style gives him sovereignty over the styles he encounters. If they have something to teach him, he may learn from them; he may also adapt them to his own objectives, but he can hardly imitate them outright.

However, there are common ingredients in every successful style of communication. It is the purpose of this chapter to identify a number of these ingredients, plus others that may be useful. In chapter 4, I discussed and gave examples of the larger structure of the sermon; here, I will deal with the "microstructures," thus moving from points to words. We shall focus both on what to say and how to say it.

I. POINTS AND PARAGRAPHS

What should you do with what has been variously called a subthesis, a division, a point, an assertion, or a topic sentence? You say, "I have good points for my sermon. Where do I go from there?"

Definition   The first thing you can do is to define the terms of the assertion, especially if it is not immediately clear to most of your listeners. Sometimes you will need to do no more than reword the assertion. Occasionally, however, terms that are unfamiliar to the average audience have to be used. So make sure that the words you use mean the same to your hearers as they mean to you. No harm comes from using such ancient or esoteric theological terms as justification, sanctification, and adoption, so long as you take time to tell what you mean by them. These honorable words can reenter the vocabulary of popular devotion if preachers respectfully introduce them to congregations who have never heard them or have never stopped to ponder their meaning.

Restatement   The task of definition can often be performed by repeating your idea without formal definitions. When this is done in typical Hebrew poetry, particularly in the Psalms, it is called *parallelism*. Informally we use it every day in communicating with one another. Sometimes we repeat what we have said in exactly the same words; sometimes, in different words. George W. Truett possessed the remarkable ability to phrase and rephrase the same idea with many intriguing variations.

A preacher may repeat himself because he is stalling for time to gather his thoughts or because age has purloined his concentration or memory. But he may do so more worthily. One may deliberately restate his ideas in order to make them clearer, more digestible, more impressive, or more stimulating. Strictly speaking, restatement adds nothing to the original assertion; it says it again, either in the same words or in different ones. Observe how Brooks uses restatement:

> What is striking in the narrative is this, that when Jesus is moved by their suffering, He is moved in all His nature. Every part of Him is stirred. Not merely His emotions and His impulses, so that He is eager to relieve at once the wretchedness which looks up to Him out of their famished eyes, but His wisdom is stirred. All the principles of His life start into action together, all His care and pity. His care and pity for the soul as well as for the body move at once.[3]

Restatement may serve a number of purposes: to hold the same idea for a greater length of time before the hearers; to summarize a paragraph while reiterating the idea contained in the topic sentence; to provide a kind of symphonic refrain; or to sum up the central idea or ideas developed in sections of the sermon or in the sermon as a whole. Sir Winston Churchill indicated that this was his technique of speechmaking. He chose an idea and hit it again and again, like a pile driver, until he had driven it home. Rudolf Flesch wisely said, "Don't disparage redundancy: it's the only weapon you have against the semantic noise that surrounds you."[4]

Examples Definition and restatement, though essential, do not suffice. Examples, actual instances, are needed. In the words of H. H. Farmer, "abstractness in some ways is the greatest curse of all our preaching."[5] Examples lend the needed concreteness. An actual instance of what you are talking about is, as the Chinese would say, worth a thousand words. Citing a case fosters clarity, credibility, sympathy (or revulsion), and stimulus for action. A sermon gains strength when the one who hears it can visualize the particular content of its generalizations. What is included in the assertion? What does it imply in terms of personal experience—that which one sees, hears, feels, smells, tastes?

In a sermon on the cost of discipleship, Professor Farmer asserts, "You cannot taste every experience and see what it is like, for every experience you have cuts out the possibility of others." With three *general* examples he then shows what this means:

> If you live on rich foods you spoil your palate for simple ones. If you read bad books you restrict and starve your capacities for appreciating good. If you indulge in vice you coarsen and vitiate your soul so that it becomes impossible for it to have the full experience and joy of virtue.[6]

In a narrative portion of one of my own sermons, note first the assertion negatively stated—what the prophet did not expect—then, the general examples—what the prophet actually envisaged:

> King Zedekiah sent two emissaries to Jeremiah the prophet, and they said, "Inquire of the Lord for us . . . ; perhaps the Lord will deal with us according to all his wonderful deeds, and will make [the enemy] withdraw from us" (Jer. 21:2 RSV). But the prophet saw no heavenly wonder in the offing. He saw the

Chaldeans pouring through the rubble of a broken city wall. He saw firebrands carried from house to house by shouting ravagers. He saw frightened old people and children fleeing like foxes from their hiding places. He saw the land outside stripped of men and cattle. The saddened prophet saw inevitable destruction.[7]

General examples may be impressive, but *specific* examples often carry a greater weight of conviction. Why? They call names. They point to definite places. They give dates. The convincing force of such examples is clear in this excerpt from a sermon by Harry Emerson Fosdick. He argues that babies are more decisive than battles:

> The year 1809, for example, was one of the most discouraging in Europe's history. Napoleon was dominant, as Hitler is now. His battles and victories were the absorbing news, and evil as our times are, I suspect that to those who lived then, 1809 seemed as bad or worse. But think of what was going on in 1809 that was not in the news at all. In that year Charles Darwin was born. In that year Gladstone was born, and Tennyson, and Edgar Allen Poe, and Oliver Wendell Holmes, and Cyrus McCormick, the inventor of the harvester, and Mendelssohn. At the very least, one must say that the world was not as hopeless as it looked.[8]

Another useful type of example is the *hypothetical*. It offers a wide range of possibilities to the preacher who knows people as the human beings that they are. The preacher observes; he reflects on what he has seen and heard and felt. Then, his spiritual and psychological insights clothe themselves in the form of narrative description and analysis. Like Brooks, he begins his hypothetical example somewhat like this:

> There is in a community a man of large, rich character, whose influence runs everywhere. . . .
> What shall we make of some man rich in attainments and in generous desires, well educated, well behaved, who has trained himself to be a light and help to other men, and who, now that his

> training is complete, stands in the midst of his fellow-men completely dark and helpless? . . .
>
> Think about a man who does something which you choose to call a piece of superfluous mercantile honesty.[9]

After every such introductory sentence a narrative mingled with analysis unfolds, concretizing a significant idea and thus clarifying it.

In a typical graphic passage, Helmut Thielicke is instructive:

> Perhaps I am a young person who doesn't even know where to begin with Jesus. All I have is a great hunger and thirst and many questions in my heart. And because I'm very helpless, I poke around in Nietzsche, repeat a couple of verses by Gottfried Benn, nibble a bit in Sartre, and even crib a little—and why not—from the New Testament. Let's see if something strikes my fancy, if something speaks to me! What else should I do in my helplessness except let everything pass in review before me? And while I do that (perhaps over a cigarette, lying on the rug, or slouching on the couch), and while everything is still cloudy and confused, Jesus stands there opposite me, beholds me and loves me. Everything that I do—and even if it is utterly false, and even though I persist in pushing the wrong buttons—everything that I do is surrounded and lifted up and carried by this love. I never escape from the gravitational field of this loving glance.[10]

The value of the hypothetical example is in ratio to its verisimilitude, that is, its likeness to truth. One can suppose something ridiculous or, on the contrary, something that has the ring of reality. The purpose of the example is to show what truth is or is like; therefore, it must at least *seem* to be authentic in order to do its work. The preacher will not attempt, of course, to deceive anyone as to the hypothetical character of the example. The style of presentation—"Here is a man . . ."—takes care of that. However, the preacher may know such a person, or the person may be a composite of many such individuals that he has known, including himself.

Illustrations   Illustrations are of a different order. They are valuable as a form of support because they throw light on a theme or an idea, and with the light comes warmth, perhaps, as well. Examples are actual instances or cases that demonstrate a truth; illustrations are comparisons or stories that in some way resemble an aspect of a truth, help to clarify it, and thus serve to inform or move the hearer.

The *simile* is a form of illustration, "a declaration that one thing resembles another."[11] The psalmist tells us that the godly man is "like a tree planted by streams of water," that the ungodly are "like chaff which the wind drives away." It is said of Jesus in Gethsemane that "his sweat became like great drops of blood falling down upon the ground" (RSV m).

Archbishop Fulton J. Sheen has made impressive use of simile in his sermons and addresses. For example:

> As a baby's cry would be meaningless in a universe without a mother's love; so our restlessness with the way we are would be meaningless without the love of God![12]

> You feel like a fish on top of the Empire State Building; somehow or other you are outside of your environment. . . . You feel yourself like a clock that has all the works and still will not "go," because you have broken a mainspring.[13]

> The world, and the things that are in it, will one day, like an Arab's tent, be folded away. There is nothing that endures but God![14]

The *analogy* is also a comparison, but it is a fuller comparison, "showing or implying several points of similarity."[15] This is a type of illustration frequently used by Henry Ward Beecher, and he was always on the lookout for an apt analogy. The wrought iron in a cathedral at Nuremberg, a garden and the seeds, clouds and sunshine, the ocean, a judge and a father, a prospector, a navigator, machinery, fermentation, eagles and sparrows—such were the materials that Beecher used to fashion images of truth. Canon Gordon W. Ireson said that he had made it a systematic practice for years to supply his own illustrations when reading a theological book: "Suppose I were trying to teach this truth to others; how would I illustrate it? What is the point or principle involved? What is analogous to it in everyday experience?" [16]

Note Eduard Schweizer's analogy of the "hardshell":

> Many times we have to suffer very acutely until we finally quit being like a crustacean that sits in its hard shell and is always alone with its own self, caring for nothing going on around it. Isn't there a special kind of religious hardshell? Some have never observed that God is always God for all others and that he is not nearly so interested in the life of our individual souls, as in the birth of a community in which individuals think about others and practice this concern continually in intercession and thanksgiving. God is incomparably interested in that. [17]

The analogies the preacher employs do not imply, as in logic, "reasoning from parallel causes." Rather than having to do with parallel processes, objects, or events, they have to do with similarities. Used as a sermon illustration, an analogy fulfills its purpose when it utilizes something known to help someone understand something else not so well known. Thus the analogy may break down at some point and still fulfill its purpose.

The *parable* is a repeated or extended simile, and the likeness usually rests on but one point. [18] Jesus, for instance, prefaced many of his parables with the formula, "The kingdom of heaven is like . . ." Thus he compared the kingdom of heaven to a grain of mustard seed, leaven, hidden treasure, a merchant in search of fine pearls, a net, and so on (cf. Matt. 13). However, Jesus exercised considerable flexibility in his use of parables. Some of them, in fact, hardly conform to the above definition, for it is their revelatory character, rather than their teaching or their polemic, that is to be stressed.[19]

It is difficult to distinguish between analogy and parable. Canon Theodore O. Wedel, in *The Pulpit Rediscovers Theology*, does not attempt to do so. In what he calls "The Parable of the Flower Shop," he suggest this analogy: A man may give a dozen roses for such different purposes as: a propitiatory sacrifice—he is late for dinner with a doubtful excuse, and he wants to make up for his thoughtlessness; a wooing sacrifice—he hopes to establish a relationship of love with someone; a sacrifice of thanksgiving—he appreciates the undeserved love of another and wants to show it tangibly by presenting a beautiful gift. The way flowers are given enables one to understand better the drama of repentance and forgiveness once it is made clear that propitiatory sacrifice of the sort mentioned above is totally ineffective when a deep rupture in relationship has occurred and thus "grace must take the place of bargain." Wedel has concluded:

> The analogy, or parable, is, of course, but a frail human insight into the drama of the redeeming Cross of Christ. . . . All of our human analogies are but seeing through a glass darkly as we approach this ultimate mystery of the drama of redemption. Yet even when we see it only falteringly, it has the power to usher us into the forecourts of heaven.[20]

However, we must think of at least some of the parables of Jesus as the preaching itself, not as a form of support or development of an idea or assertion.

The *metaphor* is still another form of illustration. It differs from the simile in this way: the simile makes an explicit comparison; the metaphor implies a comparison. Jesus could have said of Herod, "He is like a fox," but he said, "Go and tell that fox . . ." The metaphor captures an argument in a word or a truth in the stroke of an artist's brush, a fleeting note of music, a subtle fragrance, a flavor, or a mere touch.

All verbal communication is made up of metaphors dead or alive. Probably all of our most abstract words were once pictures. Just as primitive rhythm has captured the imagination of contemporary youth, so the ancient art of verbal picture-making can enthrall moderns with appeal to something fundamental in human personality. In addition, metaphors, according to Sir Ernest Gowers, enable one "to convey briefly and vividly ideas that might otherwise need tedious exposition."[21]

To his disciples Jesus said, "You are the salt of the earth. . . . You are the light of the world." And he asked, "Why do you see the speck that is in your brother's eye, but do not notice the log that is in your own eye?" The preacher today can make his preaching more vivid by the judicious use of metaphors, taking care not to pile up too many of them in single sentences or in a series of sentences. Such a surfeit can choke the understanding. But consider the strength that such metaphors as these can add to your sentences:

> Fear drove him away.
> He exchanged the rags of self-righteousness for
>   the robe of Christ's righteousness.
> She drew the curtain on her past life.
> Faith can be eroded by the acids of indecision.

Charles W. Ferguson has made this helpful suggestion: select some profession or trade, and for practice make your metaphors from this for one entire day; then, choose another for the next day, and make your metaphors from it; continue on, changing each day and attempting to carry over your metaphors into common speech and writing.[22]

The *allegory* is an extension of the metaphor.[23] Bunyan's *Pilgrim's Progress* comes immediately to mind. Isaiah's Song of the Vineyard (Isa. 5:1-6) fulfills the requirements of the allegory, as does Jesus' description of the "true vine" (John 15:1-17).

A speaker with a flair for the dramatic might say something like the following, combining personification with allegory:

> Ah, Death, now I know who you are. I have seen you a thousand times and did not recognize you. I have lived with you every day of my life. You were calling me at every crossroads. Some day you will devour me, but not forever! "Death, thou shalt die!" . . . So Death is the unseen and uninvited guest when a child is born, when a marriage takes place, when a vocation is chosen, and most obviously when the days of our years have run their course. Death is the devourer. But this pale companion is present also when every decision between right and wrong is made, so that death may be defeated in dying or may triumph when life is bought with dishonor.

Another useful form of illustration is the *anecdote*. It is a brief incident or a longer story. It differs from the specific example in that it is undocumented. It is presumed to be true (it possesses at least verisimilitude) and probably is factual. However, nothing depends on its truth. Two little words—"they say"—in an incident that Fosdick related would no doubt satisfy historians.

> When Lincoln's body was brought from Washington to Illinois it passed through Albany and, as it was carried through the street, they say a colored woman stood upon the curb and lifted her little son as far as she could reach above the heads of the crowd and was heard to say to him, "Take a long look, honey. He died for you." So, if I could, I would lift up your spirit to see Calvary. Take a long look. He died for you.[24]

101

Reasons Though it is often sufficient merely to affirm and reaffirm the basic assertion of the paragraph, it is sometimes necessary to give reasons for what is asserted. The apostle Peter wisely counseled, "Always be prepared to make a defense to any one who calls you to account for the hope that is in you" (I Peter 3:15 RSV). With some audiences the mere mention of certain ideas presupposes an effort to deal with anticipated questions or objections. Thinking people do not make important decisions in an intellectual vacuum. Therefore, it may be necessary on some points to gather together one's best thoughts in logical support of one's ideas.

Let us suppose that the preacher questions the way in which some persons decide on a course of action; he must then give reasons for his reservations.

> Can I afford to ignore the law of the land, the teaching of Scripture, the rules of my church, and the counsel of friends and family when I face a serious moral decision? Someone might say, "Do what love tells you to do." But that is dangerous advice. For love can be defined in different ways; all of us do not mean the same thing when we use the word. Besides, even if I know what love means I may not have the needed maturity when I try to work it out in my own way: I may limit my love only to friends, family, or people of my own kind. Only a foolish misuse of situation ethics would lead me to reject the experience and wisdom of others when I make a crucial decision.

Causes or Results Another significant way of developing an assertion is that of dealing with its causes or results. Attention to causes often suggests a solution; attention to results often acts as a deterrent or as a stimulus to further action of certain kinds. The following separate paragraphs from the same sermon demonstrate both approaches:

> There are other times when the issue [of decision] will be confused. Then we are not confronted with a clear choice. We don't know, and perhaps cannot know at the moment, what is the

right course to follow. It is not a matter of our being double-minded persons, who are rightly regarded by James as unstable in all their ways. We are simply not infallible, and we do not at the moment have the wisdom to make a decision that leaves no room for doubt. . . . We may, in addition, be in a temporary state of anxiety or depression which clouds the future with a pall of gloom and almost guarantees that our decision will be warped. Nevertheless, life has to go on, and we must decide on the basis of such knowledge as we have. . . .

God gives courage to face the consequences of a right decision. Of course, we do not always know all of the consequences—good or bad—of a right decision. "If I had only known!" we sometimes lament in painful retrospect. But the three young Hebrews knew precisely what was in store for them. They knew that King Nebuchadnezzar made no idle threats.[25]

Testimony   A final form of support is testimony. After you have made your basic assertion, you can recount what others have to say about it. We use testimony for two main reasons: (1) to lend authority to our assertions and (2) to put our ideas into more striking and memorable language.

When the preacher wishes to avoid a long argument, he would often be wise to employ testimony. Your own opinion, positively stated, may not suffice. What did Jesus say about the matter? What did apostles say? The creeds and confessions? The church's respected theologians? The scientists, psychologists, and sociologists? What have ordinary men and women, who have lived through the experiences that you discuss and describe, had to say about it? Be careful to cite a source that the congregation would regard as authoritative or wise.

In a sermon by Fosdick on "The Service of Religious Faith to Mental Health," we find four citations of Scripture and quotations from Albert Einstein, George Eliot, and a representative of the French Academy.[26] All of them support the preacher's thesis: religious faith contributes to mental

103

health. Characteristically Fosdick's thought was nourished not only by the Bible, but also by modern biography and autobiography. He drew on artists, dramatists, doctors, educators, essayists, explorers, historians, inventors, journalists, lawyers, musicians, novelists, philosophers, poets, psychologists, reformers, religious leaders, scientists, sociologists, statesmen, and others. Sometimes Fosdick was served by the authority of knowledge; sometimes, by the authority of experience.

As already mentioned, testimony has value also for making an idea more impressive. Someone else expressed a thought more graphically and memorably than you, so you quote him. Who has not been moved by an apt quotation of some lines of poetry or of a stanza from a hymn? When the need to feel something is greater than the need to believe something, an impressive word of testimony can be the right catalyst to make the sermon an event.

Consider the power of testimony like this:

"Those who do not remember the past are condemned to relive it."—George Santayana

"A man with a new idea is a crank until the idea succeeds."—Mark Twain

"If fifty million people say a foolish thing, it is still a foolish thing."—Anatole France

"In Jesus, God came all the way downstairs."—Douglas V. Steere

"Stephen H. Dole in his *Habitable Planets for Man* estimates that in our Galaxy there are likely to be 600 million habitable planets, each of which already contains some form of life."—Cited by Isaac Asimov

"The worst sin towards our fellow creatures is not to hate them, but to be indifferent to them: that's the essence of inhumanity."—George Bernard Shaw

The question is, therefore: What can a preacher do with an idea for a point or a paragraph? Stated more pointedly: What can I do to fill in my sermon outline?

1. Define the terms.
2. Repeat the idea in different words.
3. Give examples or details of it.
4. Compare it with something else.
5. Give reasons for it.
6. Deal with its causes or results.
7. Tell what someone else says about it.

All of these forms of support or development appear in one or another of the broad types of composition, namely, exposition, argument, narration, and description. Continuous narration or description mostly uses examples or details, while exposition or argument may use the entire spectrum of supportive or developmental forms.

Rules for Paragraphs In any case, the development of paragraphs must be guided by certain underlying principles. First, there must be *unity*. You must deal with one main idea and one only. Confusion results when you reach out and pull in ideas that have nothing helpful to say about the topic sentence under discussion. Perhaps you should discuss these ideas, but they can be discussed later in their proper context and sequence. Next, there must be *coherence*. The sentences must tie in with each other. Sometimes sentences follow each other in an obvious sequence without the need for linking words, as in Julius Caesar's declaration: "I came. I saw. I conquered." Usually, however, the use of connectives or the repetition of words or phrases links one sentence to another. Finally, *progress* is essential. The paragraph must go somewhere. The sentences may move, as Robert Hall said of Thomas Chalmers's sermons, on hinges and not on wheels, but it is usually a mistake when this happens. Normally, each sentence should at least inch the thought along, though it may not catapult it with a great leap forward.

II. SENTENCES

How can sentences move the thought along in a paragraph or in some larger unit of thought?

Target No. I:
Clarity
Clarity of meaning is the primary aim of a sentence. What is the writer or speaker trying to tell me? If *understanding* is an important objective of the speaker, he will attempt to make his sentences crystal clear. Recently various agencies of the United States government have endeavored to train personnel to write readable reports. Anyone who has tried to understand a contract or official report can applaud such efforts. The preacher should, likewise, expect the approval of his congregation when he can state what he means in sentences that leave no doubt as to what he is attempting to say. Tolstoy, when old and famous as a writer, said, "Still I have always before me the ideal of the highest art: to be clear, simple, and accessible to all." [27]

How can clarity be achieved? Some have said, "Shorten your sentences." They have discovered that average sentence length is a significant index to clarity. The problem, however, is not so much sentence length itself as the number of ideas in the sentence. Put only one idea in each sentence. That will promote clarity and shorten a sentence at the same time. Theodore M. Bernstein, a *New York Times* editor, argues for this approach to understandability. But he would not make it a rule. Why? Two or more thoughts, like Siamese twins, may be inseparable. Also, different audiences invite different styles of presentation. "The relaxed reader who picks up The Times Magazine," noted Bernstein, "is a different man from the coffee-gulping, subway-riding reader of the daily paper." [28]

H. Grady Davis has shown convincingly that in oral speech the longer sentence—even the very long sentence—can be entirely clear. Factors that contribute to such clarity are these: simple basic structure of the sentence; lavish use of connecting words; parallel construction of words, phrases, and clauses within the sentence; and brevity of inner parts of the sentence. [29] By contrast, the road to stylistic obscurity is paved with complicated, unconnected sentences.

Target No. II: Interest A sentence should be not only clear, but also interesting. The one who hears you speak is like a man who sits down to eat. He wants nourishment, of course. But he wants flavor too. Starch and protein are essential, but the flavors that nature and culinary art combine with these add to their attractiveness. Variety gives flavor to sentences. You might, of course, be able to communicate most of what you want to say by using simple declarative sentences. But you would sound like a first-grade reader. There is a more excellent way!

Consider these ways of gaining variety as suggested by Robert Gunning in the following variations of the sentence "Clear, interesting speaking contains all sorts of variety."

Personal: Variety will give your speaking clarity and interest.

Conditional: If you would employ variety, you would speak more interestingly.

Specific: Variety in words, sentences, tones, and structure is a key to interesting speech.

Negative: Speech which has no variety lacks sparkle and interest.

Comparison: Speech that has variety interests the hearer; speech that lacks it is dull.

107

> *Prepositional Beginning:* Without variety, speech is dull.
> *Participial:* Lacking variety, speech is uninteresting.
> *Imperative:* Put variety in what you say in order to interest your hearer.
> *Beginning with Clause:* What your hearer likes is variety; give him that and you will hold his interest.[30]

One simple, often overlooked method of gaining variety is the use of questions. The so-called rhetorical question is well known. It is really a statement in the form of a question; it implies an answer. One may say, "Isn't it true that every secret thought of ours will, in one way or another, affect our actions?" or, "Didn't Jesus face temptation all the way from the wilderness to the cross?"

Surprisingly, an entire sermon can move along on the shoulders of questions rather than on statements. A magnificent sermon by Arthur John Gossip, "When Life Tumbles In, What Then?" is organically characterized by the interrogative style. The preacher begins with a text that poses a question, letting the form of the text determine much of the form of the sermon's development. The text is Jeremiah 12:5: "If thou hast run with the footmen, and they have wearied thee, then how canst thou contend with horses? And if in the land of peace, wherein thou trustedst, they wearied thee, then how wilt thou do in the swelling of Jordan?" In a typical passage Gossip says,

> I do not understand this life of ours. But still less can I comprehend how people in trouble and loss and bereavement can fling away peevishly from the Christian faith. In God's name, fling to what? Have we not lost enough without losing that too?[31]

All questions, however, do not imply a specific answer. Some are simply a device to create curiosity and even suspense about what is to follow. These questions might go like this: "What are the three secrets of a worthwhile life?"

"Why did Jesus refuse to arbitrate a quarrel between two brothers over an inheritance?" "Pastor, what would you do if you were in my shoes?" Such questions make the sermon suggest more of a dialogue and less of a monologue.

An added factor of interest is reference to experience. This is perhaps more important than variety of sentence structure. A. E. Phillips stated it formally as a working principle in this way: "The more the speaker brings his idea within the vivid experience of the listener, the more likely will he attain his end." [32] What will cause the listener to say, "I see," "You are right," "I feel," "I will do it"?—this is the point.

<u>Target No. III: Impressiveness</u> I have insisted that a sentence should be both clear and interesting. It may be impressive also. The impressive sentence is to the plain sentence what singing is to speaking, what poetry is to prose, what dancing is to walking. [33] Purpose, audience, and occasion will determine whether and to what degree the preacher will seek to express his thoughts in a style characterized as elegant.

It would repay any speaker who wishes to achieve impressiveness through sentence structure, to make a special study of figures of speech. E. W. Bullinger catalogued over two hundred distinct figures in the Bible, some of which have from thirty to forty varieties. [34] Sheridan Baker, in *The Complete Stylist*, listed and gave examples of more than sixty that can be used today. One instance is *chiasmus*—"a crossing"—from the well-known challenge of John F. Kennedy in his inaugural address: "Ask not what your country can do for you: ask what you can do for your country." [35]

III. WORDS

Words are the atoms of the structure and superstructure of speech. They have their paramount importance for us in their molecular combinations. Yet they are individually powerful and have to be considered individually.

The Best Use of Words   Words there will be, if there are sermons. Our concern should be to make the best use of the available words to communicate our message. Usage is elementary. We recognize the appropriateness of certain words in the pulpit, and the inappropriateness of others. This is not to say that the goal for a preacher's vocabulary is what has been called "chancel speech." Not at all. Dwight L. Moody, the noted evangelist, impressed his hearers with his unaffected manner of speaking. A contemporary said that Moody talked about religion the way he used to talk about shoes when he was a shoe salesman. His disarming style charmed even highly educated hearers and compensated, to a degree, for his grammatical errors. The New Testament was written in *koinē* Greek, the language of everyday conversation, of business and commerce, and it served as a vehicle through which Jesus Christ was proclaimed to the nations. If this is true, we should not despise simple, clear, homely words even when we are speaking in a consecrated place about the Holy Scriptures to the saints of God. The language of Zion, spoken in Louisville or New York might make even Zion appear to be a very unattractive place. Fosdick once pinpointed our dilemma: "If in this pulpit today I should cry, 'O young men and women, be holy!' what a mistake! Who wants to be holy? Nevertheless, go back to the original meaning of that word 'holy'—whole, wholesome, healthy. That is what it means." [36]

Fosdick was right. However, some words need to reenter the language of the pulpit. Psychiatrist Karl Menninger rebukes us by asking in the title of his best-selling book *Whatever Became of Sin?*

Many effective writers and speakers have told us: Use the concrete word in preference to the abstract one. This is not to suggest that abstract words have no place in the sermon, even though they can be dangerous to understanding. "Why use abstractions at all?" asks Stuart Chase. "Well, why use water at all when you can drown in it? Without abstractions we could not think in a human way."[37] However, the concrete word has the value of sensory appeal; you can see it, hear it, taste it, smell it, feel it. We have no sensory reaction to words like education, skill, or opposition. We do react, however, to their more concrete mates: schools, master craftsman, and tug-of-war.

Moreover, use the specific term in preference to the general. There is more sensory appeal in talking about a basket of juicy, red Winesap apples than simply about fruit; about Billy Graham, than about a man; about the Matterhorn, than about mountains.

Still further, use the Anglo-Saxon word in preference to the Latin. The English language is largely a mixture of Anglo-Saxon and Latin. However, scholarly, bookish speech tends to make greater use of words of Latin origin; everyday speech is largely Anglo-Saxon. Here is a graphic contrast—President Franklin Roosevelt being the winner with everyday words:

> This was an order issued by James M. Landis in Washington. It read: "Such preparations shall be made as will completely obscure all Federal buildings and non-Federal buildings occupied by the Federal Government during an air raid for any period of time from visibility by reason of internal or external illumination. Such obscuration may be obtained either by blackout construction or by termination of the illumination. This will, of course, require that in building areas in which production must continue during the blackout, construction must be provided that internal illumination may continue." Mr. Roosevelt said to rewrite it this way: "Tell them that in buildings where they have to keep the work going to put something across the window. In buildings where they can afford to let the work stop for a while, turn out the lights."[38]

Transitional Words   Special attention must be given to transitional words, the words that link divisions, paragraphs, sentences, or words together. We may use such phrases as "in the second place," "on the other hand," or "besides this." We may pick up a word or phrase from the previous division, paragraph, or sentence and repeat it in order to link together the separate blocks of thought. We may conclude a section with a question that leads naturally to the next section. We may use pronouns that refer back to nouns. Or we may use demonstrative references such as "this," "that," and "such."[39] In addition, certain other words and phrases have special uses:

Addition:	and, also, too, or, nor, again, likewise, besides, moreover, furthermore, added to that, additionally
Contrast:	but, however, on the contrary, still, yet, nevertheless
Results:	so, thus, therefore, and so, consequently, hence
Reasons:	for, because, since
Emphasis:	to be sure, indeed, in truth, in fact, of course, naturally
Concession:	although, though, whereas
Time:	then, after that, afterwards, next, soon, before
Space:	inside, beside, above, below, behind, beyond, within

Epilogue

How is it possible to put all of this together—paragraphs, sentences, and words—and make something meaningful out of it? Turning the suggestions in this book into rigid laws to be memorized and self-consciously applied will not do it. As

Henri d'Espine put it, "We need not so much to be formed as to be freed, so that at last we become simple and true."[40]

I hope, therefore, that what I have written will help you to understand better what you are presently doing, to see its weaknesses and its strengths, to diminish the weaknesses and augment the strengths. Perhaps many of the conclusions shared here could be reached by trial and error, making such a book as this unnecessary. On the other hand, this presentation of the benefits of the trials and errors of others should enable the serious reader to progress more rapidly in his development as a preacher.

Let me conclude with these final suggestions, which, if followed, will give to the contents of this book its maximum value:

1. *Read widely.* The Bible and the best sermonic literature are important, but so is literature of many varieties.

2. *Analyze what you read.* Bishop Whately's advice is excellent: "Let an author study the best models—mark their beauties of style, and dwell upon them. . . ; but let him never, *while writing,* think of any beauties of style; but content himself with such as may occur spontaneously."[41]

3. *Imitate.* R. V. Cassill, a widely published author and a teacher of writing, says:

> To anyone who truly fears that a little indoor imitation will set him in a rut he can't break out of, or set his foot on a path that will lead inevitably to embezzlement and counterfeiting U.S. currency, I must say, for heaven's sake, don't do it. But I strongly believe that those with enough equanimity to try a few imitations now and then will learn something about their craft that can hardly be learned so quickly in any other way.[42]

4. *Practice.* You may never want to read off a sermon in the pulpit and probably should not. However, to put on paper what you might say can place at your command words and

expressions that will impress themselves upon you and become available in your extemporaneous speaking. Consider this wise counsel of W. Boyd Carpenter, an eminent British preacher:

> Write as if you were writing a letter to a friend rather than as if you were writing an essay. I mean put the personal feeling, personal interest, and personal conviction into it. Try and realise that your object is to persuade, to instruct, to help, and to edify. You are not writing for a professor's eye; there is no prize at stake, except this—the prize of being able to help some anxious, sorrowful, or perplexed heart. Let your wish be to say what you have to say so that it may bring food to that hungry heart, and you will surely fall into a natural and unaffected style of address.[43]

The advice of Edward J. Hegarty in *How to Write a Speech* is simply this: "Write it to Joe."[44]

Another way of proceeding is to say your sermon aloud, composing as you go. Francisque Sarcey, a popular French lecturer, recommended a method of composition which is almost wholly oral. He would begin by walking and talking. "A lecture is never prepared," he said, "except while walking. The movement of the body lashes the blood and aids the movement of the mind."[45] Selecting a theme, he would imagine himself before an audience and then begin improvising. He would forge ahead until he had exhausted his thoughts on the theme. Then he would begin again, repeating the process as many as twenty times, if necessary, until the ideas were clarified, illustrated, and arranged in his mind and ready for presentation.

A similar procedure for sermon-making is recommended by Clyde E. Fant in his *Preaching for Today*. This method has special merit, I should think, for preachers who have had considerable experience already with pen and paper, or for preachers who regularly write materials other than sermons. For the illustrious pulpit orator Henry Ward Beecher, learning to preach was not an either/or matter between writing and oral composition. Speaking to a group of preachers, he said,

> I can say, for your encouragement, that while illustrations are as natural to me as breathing, I use fifty now to one in the early years of my ministry. For the first six or eight years, perhaps, they were comparatively few and far apart. But I developed a tendency that was latent in me, and educated myself in that respect; and that, too, by study and practice, by hard thought, and by a great many trials, both with the pen, and extemporaneously by myself, when I was walking here and there.[46]

5. *Go public.* Do this even before you are "perfect." An old saying goes, "The only way to learn to preach is by preaching." Do not let your first humiliating blunders discourage you; let them teach you. Remember: if you are a biblical preacher in the truest sense, it is not your own opinions that you preach. You are preaching the word of God. He has a stake in what you do, and you can expect his patience, his forgiveness, and his help. In the words of the apostle Paul,

> Thanks be to God, who in Christ always leads us in triumph, and through us spreads the fragrance of the knowledge of him everywhere. For we are the aroma of Christ to God among those who are being saved and among those who are perishing, to one a fragrance from death to death, to the other a fragrance of life to life. (II Cor. 2:14-16a RSV)

115

NOTES

1. Amos N. Wilder, *Early Christian Rhetoric: The Language of the Gospel* (Cambridge: Harvard University Press, 1971), p. 118.

2. Georges-Louis LeClerc de Buffon, *Discours sur le Style.*

3. Phillips Brooks, *The Candle of the Lord* (London: Macmillan & Co., 1905), p. 128.

4. Rudolf Flesch, *How to Make Sense* (New York: Harper & Brothers, 1954), p. 152.

5. Herbert H. Farmer, *The Servant of the Word* (London: The Religious Book Club, 1941), p. 99.

6. *Idem., The Healing Cross* (London: Nisbet and Co., 1938), p. 50.

7. James W. Cox, *Survey*, September 1962, p. 19.

8. Harry Emerson Fosdick, *Living Under Tension* (New York: Harper & Brothers, 1941), pp. 222-23.

9. Brooks, *Candle of the Lord*, pp. 2, 9, 26.

10. Helmut Thielicke in Franklin H. Littell, ed., *Sermons to Intellectuals* (New York: The Macmillan Co., 1963), pp. 97–98.

11. E. W. Bullinger, *Figures of Speech Used in the Bible* (Grand Rapids: Baker Book House, 1974), p. 726.

12. Fulton J. Sheen, *The Love that Waits for You* (Washington: National Council of Catholic Men, 1950), p. 32.

13. *Idem., Preface to Religion* (New York: P. J. Kenedy & Sons, 1946), p. 38.

14. *Idem., The Fulton J. Sheen Treasury* (New York: Popular Library, n.d.), p. 340.

15. Porter G. Perrin, *An Index to English* (Chicago: Scott, Foresman and Company, 1939), p. 388.

16. Gordon W. Ireson, *How Shall They Hear?* (London: S.P.C.K., 1958), p. 99.

17. Eduard Schweizer, *God's Inescapable Nearness*, trans. James W. Cox (Waco: Word Books, 1971), p. 81.

18. Bullinger, *Figures of Speech in the Bible*, p. 751.

19. Cf. Wilder, *Early Christian Rhetoric*, pp. 72–73.

20. Theodore O. Wedel, *The Pulpit Rediscovers Theology* (Greenwich, Conn.: Seabury Press, 1956), pp. 100–105.

21. Ernest Gowers, *The Complete Plain Words* (Baltimore: Penguin Books, 1954), p. 113.

22. Charles W. Ferguson, *Say It with Words* (New York: Alfred A. Knopf, 1959), pp. 57–58.

23. Bullinger, *Figures of Speech in the Bible*, p. 748.

24. Harry Emerson Fosdick, *The Hope of the World* (New York: Harper & Brothers Publishers, 1933), p. 230.

25. James W. Cox, "What Can We Expect from God in a Crisis?" unpublished sermon.

26. Harry Emerson Fosdick, *Riverside Sermons* (New York: Harper & Brothers, 1958), pp. 94–102.

27. Quoted in *Christian Science Monitor*, April 9, 1970, from *Talks with Tolstoy*, by A. B. Goldenweizer. trans. S. S. Koteliansky and V. Woolf (New York: Horizon Press).

28. Theodore M. Bernstein, *Watch Your Language* (Manhasset, N. Y.: Channel Press, 1958), pp. 116.

29. Henry Grady Davis, *Design for Preaching* (Philadelphia: Fortress Press, 1958), pp. 282–92.

30. Robert Gunning, *The Technique of Clear Writing*, 2nd ed. (New York: McGraw Hill Book Company, 1968), pp. 175–76.

31. Arthur John Gossip, *The Hero in Thy Soul* (New York: Charles Scribner's Sons, 1933), p. 110.

32. Arthur Edward Phillips, *Effective Speaking* (Chicago: The Newton Company, 1914), p. 33.

33. Richard Whately, *Elements of Rhetoric* (Carbondale, Ill.: Southern Illinois University Press, 1963), pp. 335–37.

34. Bullinger, *Figures of Speech in the Bible*, p. ix.

35. Sheridan Baker, *The Complete Stylist* (New York: Thomas Y. Crowell Co., 1966), p. 326.

36. Fosdick, *Hope of the World*, p. 51.

37. Stuart Chase, *Power of Words* (New York: Harcourt, Brace and Company, 1954), p. 142.

38. Leo Kirschbaum, *Clear Writing* (Cleveland: Meridian Books, The World Publishing Co., 1950), p. 200, quoting "What *Newsweek* Wants," published by *Newsweek*, pp. 10–11.

39. Cf. Thomas H. Cain, *Common Sense About Writing* (Englewood Cliffs: Prentice-Hall, 1967), p. 72.

40. Henri d'Espine, "Comment proclamer le message?" *Sinn und Wesen der Verkündigung* (Zürich: Evangelischer Verlag A. G. Zollikon, 1941), p. 71.

41. Whately, *Elements of Rhetoric*, pp. 337–38.

42. R. V. Cassill, *Writing Fiction*, 2nd ed., (Englewood Cliffs: Prentice-Hall, 1975), p. 38.

43. W. Boyd Carpenter, *Lectures on Preaching* (London: Macmillan & Co., 1895), pp. 149–150.

44. Edward J. Hegarty, *How to Write a Speech* (New York: McGraw-Hill Book Company, 1951), pp. 38–40.

45. Francisque Sarcey, *Recollections of Middle Life*, trans. Elisabeth Luther Cary (London: William Heinemann, 1893), p. 157.

46. Henry Ward Beecher, *Lectures on Preaching* (New York: J. B. Ford and Co., 1872), p. 175.

APPENDIXES

APPENDIX A

EXAMPLES OF SERMON PRELIMINARIES

Title:
"Your Best Friend"

Lesson:
Luke 4:14-19, 31-44

Text:
Luke 4:18-19

Central Idea:
Jesus Christ has come to help all kinds of people.

General End:
To explain.

Specific Intent:
To help this congregation *to understand* that Jesus Christ has come to help all kinds of people.

Title:
"Where Is Jesus Christ Now?"

Lesson:
Acts 1:1-5

Text:
Acts 1:3

Central Idea:
Jesus Christ is our living Lord.

General End:
To convince.

Specific Intent:
To help this congregation *to believe* that Jesus Christ is our living Lord.

Title:
"A Different Kind of King"

Lesson:
Matthew 1:18-25

Text:
Same.

Central Idea:
The true meaning of Christmas may be known only in its inner and spiritual qualities.

General End:
To revitalize.

Specific Intent:
To lead this congregation *to experience anew* the true meaning of Christmas.

Title:
"The Right Time for God"

Lesson:
Isaiah 55:6-13

Text:
Isaiah 55:6-7

Central Idea:
There is a supremely appropriate time to be converted.

General End:
To actuate.

Specific Intent:
To help the uncommitted in this congregation *to decide* to seek the Lord now.

APPENDIX B

GUIDING PRINCIPLES FOR THE INTERPRETATION OF THE BIBLE

as accepted by the Ecumenical Study Conference, held at Wadham College, Oxford, from June 29th to July 5th, 1949

Our conference has endeavoured, on the basis of the work of earlier conferences, to develop specific principles of interpretation, for the use of the Bible in relation to social and political questions. The Christian's authority lies in the will of God. It is agreed that the Bible stands in a unique position in mediating that will to us. In our study together we have used Jer. 7.1-15 as a test case in discovering the extent of agreement in the application of hermeneutical principles. We have found a measure of agreement that surprised us all. We submit the following statements as a general consensus:

I. *The necessary theological presuppositions of Biblical interpretation*

(a) It is agreed that the Bible is our common starting point, for there God's Word confronts us, a Word which humbles the hearers so that they are more ready to listen and to discuss than they are to assert their own opinions.

(b) It is agreed that the primary message of the Bible concerns God's gracious and redemptive activity for the saving of sinful man that he might create in Jesus Christ a people for himself. In this, the Bible's central concern, an authoritative claim is placed upon man and he is called upon

From *Biblical Authority for Today*, Alan Richardson and W. Schweitzer, eds. (London: SCM Press, 1951), pp. 240-44.

to respond in faith and obedience throughout the whole of his life and work. The law of love has always a binding and compelling hold upon us, and in it we encounter the inescapable will of God. On the other hand, in the more specific laws provided for the detailed organisation of the social life of a people who lived under conditions different from our own, we should through reverent and serious study seek to distinguish in the light of God's revelation in Christ the permanently binding from that of purely local and temporal significance.

(c) It is agreed that the starting point of the Christian interpreter lies within the redeemed community of which by faith he is a member.

(d) It is agreed that the centre and goal of the whole Bible is Jesus Christ. This gives the two Testaments a perspective in which Jesus Christ is seen both as the fulfilment and the end of the Law.

(e) It is agreed that the unity of the Old and the New Testaments is not to be found in any naturalistic development, or in any static identity, but in the ongoing redemptive activity of God in the history of one people, reaching its fulfilment in Christ. Accordingly it is of decisive importance for hermeneutical method to interpret the Old Testament in the light of the total revelation in the person of Jesus Christ, the Incarnate Word of God, from which arises the full Trinitarian faith of the Church.

(f) It is agreed that allegorical interpretations which were not intended by the Biblical authors are arbitrary and their use may be a disservice to the proper recognition of Biblical authority. But Christian exegesis has been justified in recognising as divinely established a certain correspondence between some events and teachings of the Old and of the New Testament.

(g) It is agreed that, although we may differ in the manner in which tradition, reason and natural law may be used in the interpretation of Scripture, any teaching that clearly contradicts the Biblical position cannot be accepted as Christian.

II. *The interpretation of a specific passage*

(a) It is agreed that one must start with an historical and critical examination of the passage. This includes:

1. The determination of the text;
2. The literary form of the passage;
3. The historical situation, the *Sitz im Leben*;
4. The meaning which the words had for the original author and hearer or reader;
5. The understanding of the passage in the light of its total context and the background out of which it emerged.

(b) It is agreed that in the case of an Old Testament passage, one must examine and expound it in relation to the revelation of God to Israel both before and after its own period. Then the interpreter should turn to the New Testament in order to view the passage in that perspective. In this procedure the Old Testament passage may receive limitation and correction, and it may also disclose in the light of the New Testament a new and more profound significance, unknown to the original writer.

(c) It is agreed that in the case of a New Testament passage one should examine it in the light of its setting and context; then turn to the Old Testament to discover its background in God's former revelation. Returning again to the New Testament one is able to see and expound the passage in the light of the whole scope of *Heilsgeschichte*. Here our understanding of a New Testament passage may be deepened through our apprehension of the Old.

III. *The discovery of the Biblical teaching on a specific social or political issue*

(a) It is agreed that one must begin with a direct study of the Biblical text in relation to a given problem; otherwise the general principles which we establish will reflect more the presuppositions of our own time than the message of the Bible. Only then may we safely deduce applications for our own situation.

(b) It is agreed that in examining a particular modern problem we should begin with the New Testament teaching. In the light of this we should consider the Old Testament evidence as well, in order to view the problem in the light of God's total revelation. In following this procedure, historical differences in the various parts of Scripture must not be overlooked; otherwise the amassing of various texts may be done in too facile a manner and the Bible made to present a united witness on a topic which in fact it does not do. Furthermore, care should be used to see the correct proportions so that too much emphasis may not be placed on a single passage and the correct Biblical perspective be lost.

(c) It is agreed that the Biblical teaching on social and political issues must be viewed in the light of the tension between life in the kingdoms of this world and participation in the Kingdom of God. While there has not been time in this conference to explore our understanding of the relation of ethics to eschatology,[1] we are agreed that the scriptural teaching of the two ages has an important bearing upon the way in which a specific social or political issue is to be interpreted.

1. See on this problem the report of two previous ecumenical study conferences (London, 1946, and Bossey, 1947), *From the Bible to the Modern World* (published by the Study Department of the World Council of Churches, Geneva).

IV. *The application of the Biblical message to the modern world*

(a) It is agreed that if we are to receive the guidance of the Holy Spirit through the Scriptures, we must discover the degree to which our particular situation is similar to that which the Bible presents. It must be remembered that absolute identity of situation is never found, and therefore the problem of adaptation becomes acute. Nevertheless in each new situation we must allow ourselves to be guided by the Bible to a knowledge of the will of God.

(b) It is agreed that the Bible speaks primarily to the Church, but it also speaks through the Church to the world inasmuch as the whole world is claimed by the Church's Lord. The Church can best speak to the world by becoming the Church remade by the Word of God.

(c) It is agreed that in applying the Biblical message to our day, interpreters diverge because of differing doctrinal and ecclesiastical traditions, differing ethical, political, and cultural outlooks, differing geographical and sociological situations, differing temperaments and gifts. It is, however, an actual experience within the Ecumenical Movement, that when we meet together, with presuppositions of which we may be largely unconscious, and bring these presuppositions to the judgment of Scripture, some of the very difficulties are removed which prevent the Gospel from being heard. Thus the Bible itself leads us back to the living Word of God.

MEMBERS OF THE CONFERENCE

Professor C. T. Craig, Madison, N.J., U.S.A.
Professor V. E. Devadutt, Serampore, Bengal, India
Professor C. H. Dodd, Cambridge, England
Professor W. Eichrodt, Basel, Switzerland
Professor G. Florovsky, New York, U.S.A.

Professor J. Marsh, Oxford, England
Dr. G. Mayeda, Japan
D. L. Munby, Oxford, England
Professor N. W. Porteous, Edinburgh, Scotland
Canon A. Richardson, Durham, England (Chairman)
Professor E. Schlink, Heidelberg, Germany
Dr. W. Schweitzer, Geneva, Switzerland (Secretary)
Rev. O. S. Tomkins, London, England
Dr. T. F. Torrance, Aberdeen, Scotland
Professor L. T. Trinterud, Chicago, U.S.A.
Professor G. E. Wright, Chicago, U.S.A.

PRESENT ONLY ON THE LAST DAYS

Bishop A. Nygren, Lund, Sweden
Professor G. Staehlin, Erlangen, Germany

YOUTH DELEGATES

A. Adegbola, Nigeria
J. A. Atger, Saint-Martin-le-Vinoux par Grenoble, France
N. S. Booth, Boston, U.S.A.
J. Gibbs, Preston, England

APPENDIX C

LECTIONARY FOR THE CHRISTIAN YEAR

This lectionary is a table of carefully chosen lessons from the Bible. For each Sunday of the year, beginning with Advent, and for several other special days, there is one lesson from the Old Testament and there are two from the New.

A three-year cycle gives a comprehensive sweep of the Bible and its major teachings. The first, second, and third years are designated by the letters A, B, and C. To keep in step with what others are doing, you may determine which series to use by beginning the B series with Advent in a year whose last two digits are divisible by three. For example, 1975 calls for the B series to begin with the first Sunday of Advent 1975. The C series will follow in 1976, and the proper sequence will begin again with A in 1977.

These lessons are being used by several Christian denominations, and helpful exegetical and homiletical materials specifically related to them are as follows:

Preaching the New Lectionary: The Word of God for the Church Today. Reginald H. Fuller. Collegeville, Minn.: The Liturgical Press, 1974.

Proclamation: Aids for Interpreting the Lessons of the Christian Year. 24 vols.; Philadelphia: Fortress Press, 1973, 1974, 1975.

ADVENT

A four-week period in which the church joyfully remembers the coming of Christ and eagerly looks forward to his coming again. Beginning with the Sunday nearest November 30, the season is observed for the four Sundays prior to Christmas.

Sunday or Festival	Year	First Lesson	Second Lesson	Gospel
1st Sunday in Advent	A	Isa. 2:1-5	Rom. 13:11-14	Matt. 24:36-44
	B	Isa. 63:16 to 64:4	I Cor. 1:3-9	Mark 13:32-37
	C	Jer. 33:14-16	I Thess. 5:1-6	Luke 21:25-36
2d Sunday in Advent	A	Isa. 11:1-10	Rom. 15:4-9	Matt. 3:1-12
	B	Isa. 40:1-5, 9-11	II Peter 3:8-14	Mark 1:1-8
	C	Isa. 9:2, 6-7	Phil. 1:3-11	Luke 3:1-6
3d Sunday in Advent	A	Isa. 35:1-6, 10	James 5:7-10	Matt. 11:2-11
	B	Isa. 61:1-4, 8-11	I Thess. 5:16-24	John 1:6-8, 19-28 ●
	C	Zeph. 3:14-18	Phil. 4:4-9	Luke 3:10-18
4th Sunday in Advent	A	Isa. 7:10-15	Rom. 1:1-7	Matt. 1:18-25
	B	II Sam. 7:8-16	Rom. 16:25-27	Luke 1:26-38
	C	Micah 5:1-4	Heb. 10:5-10	Luke 1:39-47
Christmas Eve	A	Isa. 62:1-4	Col. 1:15-20	Luke 2:1-14
	B	Isa. 52:7-10	Heb. 1:1-9	John 1:1-14
	C	Zech. 2:10-13	Phil. 4:4-7	Luke 2:15-20

CHRISTMASTIDE

The festival of the Birth of Christ, the celebration of the incarnation. A twelve-day period from December 25 to January 5, which may include either one or two Sundays after Christmas.

Sunday or Festival	Year	First Lesson	Second Lesson	Gospel
Christmas Day	A	Isa. 9:2, 6-7	Titus 2:11-15	Luke 2:1-14
	B	Isa. 62:6-12	Col. 1:15-20	Matt. 1:18-25
	C	Isa. 52:6-10	Eph. 1:3-10	John 1:1-14

CHRISTMASTIDE—Continued

Sunday or Festival	Year	First Lesson	Second Lesson	Gospel
1st Sunday After Christmas	A	Eccl. 3:1-9, 14-17	Col. 3:12-17	Matt. 2:13-15, 19-23
	B	Jer. 31:10-13	Heb. 2:10-18	Luke 2:25-35
	C	Isa. 45:18-22	Rom. 11:33 to 12:2	Luke 2:41-52
2d Sunday After Christmas	A	Prov. 8:22-31	Eph. 1:15-23	John 1:1-5, 9-14
	B	Isa. 60:1-5	Rev. 21:22 to 22:2	Luke 2:21-24
	C	Job 28:20-28	I Cor. 1:18-25	Luke 2:36-40

EPIPHANY

A season marking the revelation of God's gift of himself to all men. Beginning with the day of Epiphany (January 6), this season continues until Ash Wednesday, and can include from four to eight Sundays.

Sunday or Festival	Year	First Lesson	Second Lesson	Gospel
Epiphany		Isa. 60:1-6	Eph. 3:1-6	Matt. 2:1-12
1st Sunday After Epiphany	A	Isa. 42:1-7	Acts 10:34-43	Matt. 3:13-17
	B	Isa. 61:1-4	Acts 11:4-18	Mark 1:4-11
	C	Gen. 1:1-5	Eph. 2:11-18	Luke 3:15-17, 21-22

(or the readings for the day of Epiphany, if observed on Sunday)

Sunday or Festival	Year	First Lesson	Second Lesson	Gospel
2d Sunday After Epiphany	A	Isa. 49:3-6	I Cor. 1:1-9	John 1:29-34
	B	I Sam. 3:1-10	I Cor. 6:12-20	John 1:35-42
	C	Isa. 62:2-5	I Cor. 12:4-11	John 2:1-12
3rd Sunday After Epiphany	A	Isa. 9:1-4	I Cor. 1:10-17	Matt. 4:12-23
	B	Jonah 3:1-5, 10	I Cor. 7:29-31	Mark 1:14-22
	C	Neh. 8:1-3, 5-6, 8-10	I Cor. 12:12-30	Luke 4:14-21
4th Sunday After Epiphany	A	Zeph. 2:3; 3:11-13	I Cor. 1:26-31	Matt. 5:1-12
	B	Deut. 18:15-22	I Cor. 7:32-35	Mark 1:21-28
	C	Jer. 1:4-10	I Cor. 13:1-13	Luke 4:22-30

EPIPHANY—Continued

Sunday or Festival	Year	First Lesson	Second Lesson	Gospel
5th Sunday After Epiphany	A	Isa. 58:7-10	I Cor. 2:1-5	Matt. 5:13-16
	B	Job 7:1-7	I Cor. 9:16-19, 22-23	Mark 1:29-39
	C	Isa. 6:1-8	I Cor. 15:1-11	Luke 5:1-11
6th Sunday After Epiphany	A	Deut. 30:15-20	I Cor. 2:6-10	Matt. 5:27-37
	B	Lev. 13:1-2, 44-46	I Cor. 10:31 to 11:1	Mark 1:40-45
	C	Jer. 17:5-8	I Cor. 15:12-20	Luke 6:17-26
7th Sunday After Epiphany	A	Lev. 19:1-2, 17-18	I Cor. 3:16-23	Matt. 5:38-48
	B	Isa. 43:18-25	II Cor. 1:18-22	Mark 2:1-12
	C	I Sam. 26:6-12	I Cor. 15:42-50	Luke 6:27-36
8th Sunday After Epiphany	A	Isa. 49:14-18	I Cor. 4:1-5	Matt. 6:24-34
	B	Hos. 2:14-20	II Cor. 3:17 to 4:2	Mark 2:18-22
	C	Job 23:1-7	I Cor. 15:54-58	Luke 6:39-45
9th Sunday After Epiphany		Use readings listed for 27th Sunday after Pentecost.		

LENT

A period of forty weekdays and six Sundays, beginning on Ash Wednesday and culminating in Holy Week. In joy and sorrow during this season, the church proclaims, remembers, and responds to the atoning death of Christ.

Sunday or Day	Year	First Lesson	Second Lesson	Gospel
Ash Wednesday	A	Joel 2:12-18	II Cor. 5:20 to 6:2	Matt. 6:1-6, 16-18
	B	Isa. 58:3-12	James 1:12-18	Mark 2:15-20
	C	Zech. 7:4-10	I Cor. 9:19-27	Luke 5:29-35
1st Sunday in Lent	A	Gen. 2:7-9; 3:1-7	Rom. 5:12-19	Matt. 4:1-11
	B	Gen. 9:8-15	I Peter 3:18-22	Mark 1:12-15
	C	Deut. 26:5-11	Rom. 10:8-13	Luke 4:1-13
2d Sunday in Lent	A	Gen. 12:1-7	II Tim. 1:8-14	Matt. 17:1-9
	B	Gen. 22:1-2, 9-13	Rom. 8:31-39	Mark 9:1-9

LENT—Continued

Sunday or Festival	Year	First Lesson	Second Lesson	Gospel
2d Sunday (cont.)	C	Gen. 15:5-12, 17-18	Phil. 3:17 to 4:1	Luke 9:28-36
3d Sunday in Lent	A	Ex. 24:12-18	Rom. 5:1-5	John 4:5-15 19-26
	B	Ex. 20:1-3, 7-8, 12-17	I Cor. 1:22-25	John 2:13-25
	C	Ex. 3:1-8, 13-15	I Cor. 10:1-12	Luke 13:1-9
4th Sunday in Lent	A	II Sam. 5:1-5	Eph. 5:8-14	John 9:1-11
	B	II Chron. 36:14-21	Eph. 2:1-10	John 3:14-21
	C	Josh. 5:9-12	II Cor. 5:16-21	Luke 15:11-32
5th Sunday in Lent	A	Ezek. 37:11-14	Rom. 8:6-11	John 11:1-4, 17, 34-44
	B	Jer. 31:31-34	Heb. 5:7-10	John 12:20-33
	C	Isa. 43:16-21	Phil. 3:8-14	Luke 22:14-30
Palm Sunday	A	Isa. 50:4-7	Phil. 2:5-11	Matt. 21:1-11
	B	Zech. 9:9-12	Heb. 12:1-6	Mark 11:1-11
	C	Isa. 59:14-20	I Tim. 1:12-17	Luke 19:28-40

HOLY WEEK

The week prior to Easter, during which the church gratefully commemorates the passion and death of Jesus Christ.

Day of Holy Week	Year	First Lesson	Second Lesson	Gospel
Monday		Isa. 50:4-10	Heb. 9:11-15	Luke 19:41-48
Tuesday		Isa. 42:1-9	I Tim. 6:11-16	John 12:37-50
Wednesday		Isa. 52:13 to 53:12	Rom. 5:6-11	Luke 22:1-16
Maundy Thursday	A	Ex. 12:1-8 11-14	I Cor. 11:23-32	John 13:1-15
	B	Deut. 16:1-8	Rev. 1:4-8	Matt. 26:17-30
	C	Num. 9:1-3, 11-12	I Cor. 5:6-8	Mark 14:12-26
Good Friday	A	Isa. 52:13 to 53:12	Heb. 4:14-16; 5:7-9	John 19:17-30
	B	Lam. 1:7-12	Heb. 10:4-18	Luke 23:33-46
	C	Hos. 6:1-6	Rev. 5:6-14	Matt. 27:31-50

133

EASTERTIDE

A fifty-day period of seven Sundays, beginning with Easter, the festival of Christ's resurrection. Ascension Day, forty days after Easter, is celebrated to affirm that Jesus Christ is Lord of all times and places.

Sunday or Festival	Year	First Lesson	Second Lesson	Gospel
Easter	A	Acts 10:34-43	Col. 3:1-11	John 20:1-9
	B	Isa. 25:6-9	I Peter 1:3-9	Mark 16:1-8
	C	Ex. 15:1-11	I Cor. 15:20-26	Luke 24:13-35
2d Sunday in Eastertide	A	Acts 2:42-47	I Peter 1:3-9	John 20:19-31
	B	Acts 4:32-35	I John 5:1-6	Matt. 28:11-20
	C	Acts 5:12-16	Rev. 1:9-13, 17-19	John 21:1-14
3d Sunday in Eastertide	A	Acts 2:22-28	I Peter 1:17-21	Luke 24:13-35
	B	Acts 3:13-15, 17-19	I John 2:1-6	Luke 24:36-49
	C	Acts 5:27-32	Rev. 5:11-14	John 21:15-19
4th Sunday in Eastertide	A	Acts 2:36-41	I Peter 2:19-25	John 10:1-10
	B	Acts 4:8-12	I John 3:1-3	John 10:11-18
	C	Acts 13:44-52	Rev. 7:9-17	John 10:22-30
5th Sunday in Eastertide	A	Acts 6:1-7	I Peter 2:4-10	John 14:1-12
	B	Acts 9:26-31	I John 3:18-24	John 15:1-8
	C	Acts 14:19-28	Rev. 21:1-5	John 13:31-35
6th Sunday in Eastertide	A	Acts 8:4-8, 14-17	I Peter 3:13-18	John 14:15-21
	B	Acts 10:34-48	I John 4:1-7	John 15:9-17
	C	Acts 15:1-2, 22-29	Rev. 21:10-14, 22-23	John 14:23-29
Ascension Day		Acts 1:1-11	Eph. 1:16-23	Luke 24:44-53
17th Sunday in Eastertide	A	Acts 1:12-14	I Peter 4:12-19	John 17:1-11
	B	Acts 1:15-17, 21-26	I John 4:11-16	John 17:11-19
	C	Acts 7:55-60	Rev. 22:12-14, 16-17, 20	John 17:20-26

(or the readings for Ascension Day, if observed on Sunday)

PENTECOST

The festival commemorating the gift of the Holy Spirit to the church, and an extended season for reflecting on how God's people live under the guidance of his Spirit. The season extends from the seventh Sunday after Easter to the beginning of Advent.

Sunday	Year	First Lesson	Second Lesson	Gospel
Pentecost	A	I Cor. 12:4-13	Acts 2:1-13	John 14:15-26
(Whitsunday)	B	Joel 2:28-32	Acts 2:1-13	John 16:5-15
	C	Isa. 65:17-25	Acts 2:1-13	John 14:25-31
1st Sunday	A	Ezek. 37:1-4	II Cor. 13:5-13	Matt. 28:16-20
After Pentecost	B	Isa. 6:1-8	Rom. 8:12-17	John 3:1-8
(Trinity Sunday)	C	Prov. 8:22-31	I Peter 1:1-9	John 20:19-23
2d Sunday	A	Deut. 11:18-21	Rom. 3:21-28	Matt. 7:21-29
After Pentecost	B	Deut. 5:12-15	II Cor. 4:6-11	Mark 2:23 to 3:6
	C	I Kings 8:41-43	Gal. 1:1-10	Luke 7:1-10
3d Sunday	A	Hos. 6:1-6	Rom. 4:13-25	Matt. 9:9-13
After Pentecost	B	Gen. 3:9-15	II Cor. 4:13 to 5:1	Mark 3:20-35
	C	I Kings 17:17-24	Gal. 1:11-19	Luke 7:11-17
4th Sunday	A	Ex. 19:2-6	Rom. 5:6-11	Matt. 9:36 to 10:8
After Pentecost	B	Ezek. 17:22-24	II Cor. 5:6-10	Mark 4:26-34
	C	II Sam. 12:1-7a	Gal. 2:15-21	Luke 7:36-50
5th Sunday	A	Jer. 20:10-13	Rom. 5:12-15	Matt. 10:26-33
After Pentecost	B	Job 38:1-11	II Cor. 5:16-21	Mark 4:35-41
	C	Zech. 12:7-10	Gal. 3:23-29	Luke 9:18-24
6th Sunday	A	II Kings 4:8-16	Rom. 6:1-11	Matt. 10:37-42
After Pentecost	B	Gen. 4:3-10	II Cor. 8:7-15	Mark 5:21-43
	C	I Kings 19:15-21	Gal. 5:1, 13-18	Luke 9:51-62
7th Sunday	A	Zech. 9:9-13	Rom. 8:6-11	Matt. 11:25-30
After Pentecost	B	Ezek. 2:1-5	II Cor. 12:7-10	Mark 6:1-6
	C	Isa. 66:10-14	Gal. 6:11-18	Luke 10:1-9
8th Sunday	A	Isa. 55:10-13	Rom. 8:12-17	Matt. 13:1-17
After Pentecost	B	Amos. 7:12-17	Eph. 1:3-10	Mark 6:7-13
	C	Deut. 30:9-14	Col. 1:15-20	Luke 10:25-37

PENTECOST—Continued

Sunday	Year	First Lesson	Second Lesson	Gospel
9th Sunday After Pentecost	A	II Sam. 7:18-22	Rom. 8:18-25	Matt. 13:24-35
	B	Jer. 23:1-6	Eph. 2:11-18	Mark 6:30-34
	C	Gen. 18:1-11	Col. 1:24-28	Luke 10:38-42
10th Sunday After Pentecost	A	I Kings 3:5-12	Rom. 8:26-30	Matt. 13:44-52
	B	II Kings 4:42-44	Eph. 4:1-6, 11-16	John 6:1-15
	C	Gen. 18:20-33	Col. 2:8-15	Luke 11:1-13
11th Sunday After Pentecost	A	Isa. 55:1-3	Rom. 8:31-39	Matt. 14:13-21
	B	Ex. 16:2-4, 12-15	Eph. 4:17-24	John 6:24-35
	C	Eccl. 2:18-23	Col. 3:1-11	Luke 12:13-21
12th Sunday After Pentecost	A	I Kings 19:9-16	Rom. 9:1-5	Matt. 14:22-23
	B	I Kings 19:4-8	Eph. 4:30 to 5:2	John 6:41-51
	C	II Kings 17:33-40	Heb. 11:1-3, 8-12	Luke 12:35-40
13th Sunday After Pentecost	A	Isa. 56:1-7	Rom. 11:13-16, 29-32	Matt. 15:21-28
	B	Prov. 9:1-6	Eph. 5:15-20	John 6:51-59
	C	Jer. 38:1b-13	Heb. 12:1-6	Luke 12:49-53
14th Sunday After Pentecost	A	Isa. 22:19-23	Rom. 11:33-36	Matt. 16:13-20
	B	Josh. 24:14-18	Eph. 5:21-33	John 6:60-69
	C	Isa. 66:18-23	Heb. 12:7-13	Luke 13:22-30
15th Sunday After Pentecost	A	Jer. 20:7-9	Rom. 12:1-7	Matt. 16:21-28
	B	Deut. 4:1-8	James 1:19-25	Mark 7:1-8, 14-15, 21-23
	C	Prov. 22:1-9	Heb. 12:18-24	Luke 14:1, 7-14
16th Sunday After Pentecost	A	Ezek. 33:7-9	Rom. 13:8-10	Matt. 18:15-20
	B	Isa. 35:4-7	James 2:1-5	Mark 7:31-37
	C	Prov. 9:8-12	Philemon 8-17	Luke 14:25-33
17th Sunday After Pentecost	A	Gen. 4:13-16	Rom. 14:5-9	Matt. 18:21-35
	B	Isa. 50:4-9	James 2:14-18	Mark 8:27-35
	C	Ex. 32:7-14	I Tim. 1:12-17	Luke 15:1-32
18th Sunday After Pentecost	A	Isa. 55:6-11	Phil. 1:21-27	Matt. 20:1-16
	B	Jer. 11:18-20	James 3:13 to 4:3	Mark 9:30-37

PENTECOST—Continued

Sunday	Year	First Lesson	Second Lesson	Gospel
18th Sunday (cont.)	C	Amos 8:4-8	I Tim. 2:1-8	Luke 16:1-13
19th Sunday After Pentecost	A	Ezek. 18:25-29	Phil. 2:1-11	Matt. 21:28-32
	B	Num. 11:24-30	James 5:1-6	Mark 9:38-48
	C	Amos 6:1, 4-7	I Tim. 6:11-16	Luke 16:19-31
20th Sunday After Pentecost	A	Isa. 5:1-7	Phil. 4:4-9	Matt. 21:33-43
	B	Gen. 2:18-24	Heb. 2:9-13	Mark 10:2-16
	C	Heb. 1:1-3; 2:1-4	II Tim. 1:3-12	Luke 17:5-10
21st Sunday After Pentecost	A	Isa. 25:6-9	Phil. 4:12-20	Matt. 22:1-14
	B	Prov. 3:13-18	Heb. 4:12-16	Mark 10:17-27
	C	II Kings 5:9-17	II Tim. 2:8-13	Luke 17:11-19
22d Sunday After Pentecost	A	Isa. 45:1-6	I Thess. 1:1-5	Matt. 22:15-22
	B	Isa. 53:10-12	Heb. 5:1-10	Mark 10:35-42
	C	Ex. 17:8-13	II Tim. 3:14 to 4:2	Luke 18:1-8
23d Sunday After Pentecost	A	Ex. 22:21-27	I Thess. 1:2-10	Matt. 22:34-40
	B	Jer. 31:7-9	Heb. 5:1-6	Mark 10:46-52
	C	Deut. 10:16-22	II Tim. 4:6-8, 16-18	Luke 18:9-14
24th Sunday After Pentecost	A	Mal. 2:1-10	I Thess. 2:7-13	Matt. 23:1-12
	B	Deut. 6:1-9	Heb. 7:23-28	Mark 12:28-34
	C	Ex. 34:5-9	II Thess. 1:11 to 2:2	Luke 19:1-10
25th Sunday After Pentecost	A	S. of Sol. 3:1-5	I Thess. 4:13-18	Matt. 25:1-13
	B	I Kings 17:8-16	Heb. 9:24-28	Mark 12:38-44
	C	I Chron. 29:10-13	II Thess. 2:16 to 3:5	Luke 20:27-38
26th Sunday After Pentecost	A	Prov. 31:10-13 19-20, 30-31	I Thess. 5:1-6	Matt. 25:14-30
	B	Dan. 12:1-4	Heb. 10:11-18	Mark 13:24-32
	C	Mal. 3:16 to 4:2	II Thess. 3:6-13	Luke 21:5-19
27th Sunday After Pentecost	A	Ezek. 34:11-17	I Cor. 15:20-28	Matt. 25:31-46
	B	Dan. 7:13-14	Rev. 1:4-8	John 18:33-37
	C	II Sam. 5:1-4	I Cor. 15:20-28	Luke 23:35-43
28th Sunday After Pentecost		Use readings listed for 8th Sunday after Epiphany.		

SPECIAL DAYS

"It is also fitting that congregations celebrate such other days as recall the heritage of the reformed church, proclaim its mission, and forward its work; and such days as recognize the civic responsibilities of the people." (*Directory for Worship*, 19.04c.)

Special Day	Year	First Lesson	Second Lesson	Gospel
New Year's Eve or Day	A	Deut. 8:1-10	Rev. 21:1-7	Matt. 25:31-46
	B	Eccl. 3:1-13	Col. 2:1-7	Matt. 9:14-17
	C	Isa. 49:1-10	Eph. 3:1-10	Luke 14:16-24
Christian Unity	A	Isa. 11:1-9	Eph. 4:1-16	John 15:1-8
	B	Isa. 35:3-10	I Cor. 3:1-11	Matt. 28:16-20
	C	Isa. 55:1-5	Rev. 5:11-14	John 17:1-11
World Communion	A	Isa. 49:18-23	Rev. 3:17-22	John 10:11-18
	B	Isa. 25:6-9	Rev. 7:9-17	Luke 24:13-35
	C	I Chron. 16:23-34	Acts 2:42-47	Matt. 8:5-13
Reformation Sunday	A	Hab. 2:1-4	Rom. 3:21-28	John 8:31-36
	B	Gen. 12:1-4	II Cor. 5:16-21	Matt. 21:17-22
	C	Ex. 33:12-17	Heb. 11:1-10	Luke 18:9-14
Thanksgiving Day	A	Isa. 61:10-11	I Tim. 2:1-8	Luke 12:22-31
	B	Deut. 26:1-11	Gal. 6:6-10	Luke 17:11-19
	C	Deut. 8:6-17	II Cor. 9:6-15	John 6:24-35
Day of civic or national significance	A	Deut. 28:1-9	Rom. 13:1-8	Luke 1:68-79
	B	Isa. 26:1-8	I Thess. 5:12-23	Mark 12:13-17
	C	Dan. 9:3-10	I Peter 2:11-17	Luke 20:21-26

INDEX